FORGIVING
As We've Been
FORGIVEN

Community Practices for Making Peace

L. GREGORY JONES
& CÉLESTIN MUSEKURA

Resources for Reconciliation

series editors

EMMANUEL KATONGOLE & CHRIS RICE

IVP Books

An imprint of InterVarsity Press
Downers Grove, Illinois

InterVarsity Press
P.O. Box 1400, Downers Grove, IL 60515-1426
World Wide Web: www.ivpress.com
Email: email@ivpress.com

InterVarsity Press® is the book-publishing division of InterVarsity Christian Fellowship/USA®, a movement of students and faculty active on campus at hundreds of universities, colleges and schools of nursing in the United States of America, and a member movement of the International Fellowship of Evangelical Students. For information about local and regional activities, write Public Relations Dept., InterVarsity Christian Fellowship/USA, 6400 Schroeder Rd., P.O. Box 7895, Madison, WI 53707-7895, or visit the IVCF website at <www.intervarsity.org>.

Scripture quotations, unless otherwise noted, are from the New Revised Standard Version of the Bible, copyright 1989 by the Division of Christian Education of the National Council of the Churches of Christ in the USA. Used by permission. All rights reserved.

Design: Cindy Kiple

Images: Woman Caught in Adultery by Rick Beerhorst

ISBN 978-0-8308-3455-6

Printed in the United States of America ∞

InterVarsity Press is committed to protecting the environment and to the responsible use of natural resources. As a member of Green Press Initiative we use recycled paper whenever possible. To learn more about the Green Press Initiative, visit <www.greenpressinitiative.org>.

Library of Congress Cataloging-in-Publication Data

Jones, L. Gregory.
  Forgiving as we've been forgiven : community practices for making
peace / L. Gregory Jones and Celestin Musekura.
    p. cm.—(Resources for reconciliation)
  Includes bibliographical references (p.   ).
  ISBN 978-0-8308-3455-6 (pbk. : alk. paper)
  1. Forgiveness—Religious aspects—Christianity. I. Musekura,
Celestin. II. Title.
  BV4647.F55J67 2010
  241'.4—dc22
                                                              2010019865

P   25   24   23   22   21   20   19   18   17   16   15   14   13   12   11   10   9   8   7   6   5   4   3

Y   31   30   29   28   27   26   25   24   23   22   21   20   19   18   17   16   15   14

For our families

Contents

Series Preface

The Resources for Reconciliation Book Series

A partnership between InterVarsity Press and the Center for Reconciliation at Duke Divinity School, Resources for Reconciliation books address what it means to pursue hope in areas of brokenness, including the family, the city, the poor, the disabled, Christianity and Islam, racial and ethnic divisions, violent conflicts, and the environment. The series seeks to offer a fresh and distinctive vision for reconciliation as God's mission and a journey toward God's new creation in Christ. Each book is authored by two leading voices, one in the field of practice or grass-roots experience, the other from the academy. Each book is grounded in the biblical story, engages stories and places of pain and hope, and seeks to help readers to live faithfully—a rich mix of theology, context and practice.

This book series was born out of the mission of the Duke Divinity School Center for Reconciliation: *Advancing God's mission of reconciliation in a divided world by cultivating new leaders, communicating wisdom and hope, and connecting in outreach to strengthen leadership.* A divided world needs people with the vision, spiritual maturity and daily skills integral to the journey of reconciliation. The church needs fresh resources—a mix of biblical vision, social skills of social and historical analysis, and practical gifts of spirituality and social leadership—in order to pursue reconciliation in real places, from congregations to communities.

The ministry of reconciliation is not reserved for experts. It is the core of God's mission and an everyday call of the Christian life. These books are written to equip and stimulate God's people to be more faithful ambassadors of reconciliation in a fractured world.

For more information, email the Duke Divinity School Center for Reconciliation at reconciliation@div.duke.edu, or visit our website: <www.dukereconciliation.com>.

Emmanuel Katongole
Chris Rice
Center codirectors and series editors

Before We Get Started . . .

L . GREGORY JONES &
CÉLESTIN MUSEKURA

*T*his is a book about forgiveness—something we Christians are supposed to understand. Anyone who knows the Lord's Prayer knows that we ask to be forgiven as we forgive. But hearing the call to forgive is different than knowing how to practice forgiveness at home and in the world. Forgiveness is about more than the isolated acts and words of individuals. To forgive and be forgiven, we need communal practices and disciplines—a way of life that makes for peace. This book is about how churches and communities can cultivate the habits that make forgiveness possible on a daily basis.

We are delighted to have the opportunity to write this

book together. I (Célestin) know firsthand the challenge of forgiveness. I grew up as a Hutu in a Rwandan village that was fragmented by tribal identities that trumped every other allegiance. When my father and other family members were killed in the aftermath of Rwanda's genocide, I heard God ask for my ultimate allegiance. He said I had to forgive the killers before I knew who they were. The healing power of forgiveness in my own life inspired me to found ALARM—African Leadership and Reconciliation Ministries. With fifty-one staff in eight countries, ALARM teaches the power of forgiveness and empowers people to practice it in broken communities. It has been my joy to watch forgiveness transform the lives of thousands of people over the past fifteen years.

I (Greg) have written about forgiveness as an academic theologian and worked to make it a more central theme within the institutions that train Christian pastors and teachers. I've spent the last twenty years telling stories about people like Célestin. But I also know how important forgiveness is for people who haven't experienced traumatic violence or a national tragedy like Rwanda's genocide. We are, each of us, broken people. In every community we bump into each other, and our sharp edges wound others—even those we love most. Whether our daily focus is international affairs or raising children, each of us needs to grow in the practice of forgiveness.

So we have written this book together. This series aims to

bring together academics and practitioners. Truth be told, both of us are academics. And both of us are practitioners. Our passion for forgiveness has led us both to study and to write. But it has also propelled both of us into the work of shepherding communities of forgiveness and building institutions that embody the good news we preach. Though we come from different worlds, both geographically and denominationally, we've found we have a lot in common.

Still, our journeys have been quite different. Having grown out of different soil and walked distinct paths, our voices are different. Rather than try to make them one, we've decided to go back and forth, one chapter at a time, each of us listening to the other and building on what has already been said. As you'll see in chapter two, I (Greg) think forgiveness is a dance. This book, too, has been something of a dance. Like the Hebrew children in Babylon's furnace, we've had the sense along the way that a third person was dancing with us in the fire. God's presence has been a gift—and it has saved us.

Having come through the fire together, our minds are still filled with awe. We wonder at God's grace, both in this project and in the stories we've had the chance to tell. But we're also pleasantly surprised at the joy we've found in partnering together. It's the kind of joy that makes you want to invite someone else onto the dance floor.

So it's a pleasure to extend our hands together and welcome you onto this journey. May you find your way into a deeper understanding of forgiveness and a richer practice of life together in these pages. May you learn with all your being to forgive as you are forgiven. And may you know in your most difficult times of trial that the God of all comfort is with you in the fire.

I

The Heart of the Gospel

CÉLESTIN MUSEKURA

*I*n the hundred days of genocide between April and July 1994, my people experienced hopelessness, abandonment, despair and death. To the world, Rwanda had no hope and no possibility of a future. To the Rwandese—perpetrators, survivors and bystanders—this national tragedy literally ended our lives. For those of us who survived that cataclysmic violence, resurrection has become a necessity. Without the practice of forgiveness in a new life that we receive from Jesus Christ, we have no hope for the future.

In October 1990 the Tutsi-led Rwandan Patriotic Front (RPF) invaded their home country of Rwanda, an incident that began the tribal war between the Tutsi minority and the Hutu-led government and its Rwandan Armed Forces.

The RPF was formed in 1987 by the Tutsi refugee diaspora in Uganda whose parents fled to Uganda during the Hutu revolution of 1959. After being denied their right to return home by the Hutu political leaders, these refugees, some of whom had become Ugandan citizens, took up arms to fight for their return to Rwanda. Thus the invasion of 1990, and the start of a civil war.

Four years later, in April 1994, the unthinkable happened to friends and neighbors in my home country. Over a period of one hundred days, nearly one million people were massacred in Rwanda's genocide. Three million people fled the country and lived and died in the refugee camps in Tanzania, Democratic Republic of Congo, Burundi and Uganda. Others were able to find refuge in Kenya, Europe and America.

Even though by the end of July 1994 the genocide was officially brought to a halt by the RPF, whose members were predominantly Tutsi, revenge killings continued until 1998. In these confrontations between the newly established Tutsi government and the Hutu militia who had fled into Congo, many people in the northwestern parts of Rwanda were killed. Among the victims of these fresh waves of killings were my own relatives and members of the congregation I pastored from 1983 until 1986.

The genocide in my country took place when I was away, finishing my graduate studies at Nairobi Evangelical Graduate School of Theology (NEGST) in Kenya. Just a few days before my graduation, I was offered a job as the associate director of urban ministries support groups for Serving in Mission (SIM). My ministry consisted of training urban pastors to reach the city, especially the growing slums of the major cities in East and central Africa. Because of the large number of refugees in Nairobi who did not speak English or Swahili, I was involved in starting a congregation of Rwandan refugees there.

In October 1994 I took a trip to try to find relatives and friends who might have survived the genocide or the killing machines of dysentery and cholera in the refugee camps of the Democratic Republic of Congo. Searching for the living among the scattered, unburied bodies, I found pastors and church leaders who had survived the killings and who were mourning the loss of their wives, children, colleagues and church members. Most of these pastors, priests and church leaders were asking, "Does God care about us? Is God really all-powerful? Where was God when my wife and children were being chopped into pieces? Are we in the days of great tribulation?"

Other pastors and priests had hidden people in their churches and homes when militia came to their doors, asking for moderate Hutus or Tutsis. If they did not comply, the militia had said, their families would be destroyed with those they were hiding. Some pastors were afraid and gave up members of their congregations to be killed. They were asking questions such as, "Why did I not die with those people? Can I be forgiven for what I did? Am I of any use now? Can I be a pastor again?"

The pastors and the church as a whole were facing ethical, theological and practical questions. The surviving pastors felt that they had nothing to say about the God who had abandoned them and allowed such horrors to happen. Many of them were wondering if the God of the Bible they had believed was more powerful and stronger than the gods of their ancestors that they had stopped worshiping. God's character was brought into question due to much suffering, hopelessness and despair.

At the end of my trip, the Lord called me to leave my well-paying job and my sense of security to go back to those refugee camps in Congo, Tanzania, Uganda and Kenya. I knew I was called to the ministry of comforting, encouraging and strengthening the pastors who had survived as well as training new pastors and layleaders to replace the 70 percent of the church's leadership who were massacred during the genocide or who had gone into exile.

The biblical message of forgiveness and reconciliation was the focus of my ministry. I knew the church of Rwanda needed to be an instrument of hope, healing and restoration in the midst of hatred and animosity. The message of repentance was not a popular one, though, as it confronted the politicians and militia who had killed or encouraged others to kill. It also challenged Hutus and Tutsis both inside the refugee camps and back home in Rwanda, the majority of whom were promoting revenge, getting even, and continuing the hatred and divisions. Justice was not defined by fair judgment but rather by what people felt would give them a sense of relief, even if it meant vengeance on an innocent person from the "wrong tribe."

Even the majority of Christians did not understand where their loyalty was. Many felt as though they were Hutu or Tutsi first, then Christian second. Our ministry displeased many, and as a result I was beaten three times in the refugee camps, tortured for three-and-a-half hours at one of the police brigades and threatened constantly, along with my family. My own fellow Hutus said I was betraying my people by asking them to repent and seek forgiveness. The Tutsis hated me because I confronted them with the message of forgiveness and restoration. Yet despite the suffering and the rejection by both tribes, the Lord continued to strengthen me and my wife and started to raise others to join us in this ministry of leadership training and reconciliation.

This is how we came to start African Leadership and Reconciliation Ministries (ALARM). It was a humble and difficult beginning fifteen years ago. The clear call we heard was to engage the Christian community, the church of Rwanda that had been involved in the genocide through the sins of commission and omission, in a radical ministry of forgiveness and reconciliation. Leaders of the church needed to be trained to understand that church trumps the obligations of tribe, race and region. Together we had to become an agent of unity and reconciliation through the message of forgiveness.

THE PERSONAL TEST OF FORGIVENESS

Revenge, hatred and village killings, though not officially sanctioned, followed the mass genocide in Rwanda, continuing until 1998. Militia and former government officials armed people in the Hutu camps, inciting them toward animosity and encouraging them to go back to fight and kill the Tutsis who had taken over their properties and "their country." Both Hutu and Tutsi hardliners demonized and dehumanized each other. As the Hutu militia launched attacks across the borders from refugee camps, many members of the newly formed Rwandan Patriotic Army (RPA) engaged in indiscriminate killings of innocent civilians, women and children who did not flee the country. Both the militia and the regular army were involved in the killing and torture of those they felt were not on their side.

On Sunday, December 28, 1997, men in uniform with guns, grenades, swords and clubs went into my village and killed about seventy people, some in their homes and on their farms, others in the church where they had gathered for morning prayer. Among those killed were my father, my stepbrother, his wife and two children, and a new sister my mother had adopted in the refugee camps in Congo. Most of the people killed were neighbors, friends and members of the church that I had pastored for four years during my early years of ministry.

I was at Dallas Theological Seminary in Texas when I received a fax from Rwanda telling me about the massacre of my friends and family members. It was late in the night of January 5, 1998, when I received this terrible news. I became angry at God and started asking him where he was when my family was being butchered, and why he would not protect them after all that I had gone through in obedience to his calling. I also wanted to know who had done this terrible act against innocent peasants who had nothing to do with the power struggle between Hutus and Tutsis.

Despite all that I had said and taught, I wanted revenge against those who killed my relatives and the people I had served and loved. I found myself asking the same questions I had heard from many refugee pastors in the summer and fall of 1994. In this unguarded moment of raw emotions, God confronted me with the reality of the ministry of forgiveness and reconciliation to which he had called me. He assured me that he was there when everything took place. He also assured me that my relatives, some of whom I had led to Christ, had finished their journey well. It was not my responsibility to question where God was when they were killed and who killed them, but rather to finish the journey well like both my family and other faithful church members who were killed during and after the genocide.

That night in Dallas, the Lord confronted me with the hardest challenge of my life: "You have been teaching others about repentance and forgiveness. You do well in instructing others and leading others toward forgiveness. It is now your turn to forgive those who killed your relatives without asking where I was. It is your turn to forgive those who brutally murdered your loved ones, even before you know their names. It is up to you to make a choice: either forgive and let me take care of the rest or fail to forgive and give up your freedom, joy and peace. You can either choose to be a hypocrite who teaches what he does not practice, or you can be the wounded healer who gives the healing gift of forgiveness to the undeserving."

After teaching people the practice of forgiveness, I had to learn that the Christian view of forgiveness involves the remembrance of divine grace and God's unconditional love and mercy toward humanity. My belief in forgiveness as a technique was not enough to keep me from bitterness, revenge and resentment. I had to go deeper—to the very heart of what our faith is about.

Because of his grace, love, mercy and compassion, God performed the unimaginable act of offering the priceless sacrifice of his Son for the forgiveness of sin, even when we were still rebellious. He made us alive with Christ even when we were powerless and dead through our transgressions (Ephesians 2:5; Romans 5:6, 8). Because of this divine act, the Christian model of forgiveness stresses the granting of unconditional forgiveness to those who cause injury, pain and suffering in this life. This gracious and miraculous act of forgiveness is possible because of the conviction that

Christians should forgive unconditionally as God in Christ forgave them, and because of the Spirit's work in Christians to help them do it.

In the midst of my grief, God showed me the transforming power of forgiveness. Forgiveness didn't only have the power to transform communities; it was changing me first. Through this personal encounter, I began to pray that my pain, sorrow, emotions and grief would not blind me from seeing the grace and forgiveness I had received from God. On January 5, 1998, I learned that forgiveness can take place even in the midst of unjust suffering and pain. I also learned that forgiveness is only possible when God's power takes over my will and desire for vengeance and human justice. The lessons I learned in this encounter between my own desire for revenge and the reality of a God who forgives unconditionally and calls the forgiven into a life of forgiveness were more than I had learned in reading books on forgiveness. I understood that God's forgiveness and redemption from the bondage of sin not only save us from eternal damnation but also invite us into a new life here and now. And I learned that through forgiveness a possibility of new hope and a new future is created between the perpetrator and the victim.

I started to understand the divine way: that indeed the forgiver pays the cost of forgiveness, even when the forgiven is unaware of the price. God paid the cost of my forgiveness. While I was still a sinner, Christ died for me (Romans 5:8).

He died so that I can be forgiven. God was teaching me that I can choose to forgive regardless of the actions of the offender. I don't have to completely heal from the wounds before I forgive. The gift does not even have to be received to be a gift. Forgiveness is the gift that I have freely received and that I should unconditionally give. As a forgiven sinner, I am called to forgive. As a redeemed saint, I must not subject myself to the bondage of unforgiveness. In his grace God did not allow me to sink into unforgiveness but called me to be an instrument of hope, healing, forgiveness and reconciliation.

God wanted me to learn to live out what I preach. If I could not find grace to extend to those who had taken the lives of my loved ones, then I should not be involved in the ministry of forgiveness and reconciliation. To this end, I prayed and asked God to grant me the strength and grace to forgive the killers of my family and friends. Then I declared forgiveness to the perpetrators. God set me free, so I had to set my enemies free. This was redemption for both of us—the forgiver and the forgiven. It was redemption from anger and bitterness on my side as well as from the effects of revenge on the side of the perpetrators. But more importantly for both of us, this was redemption to the possibility of a new relationship with God for me and for my forgiven friends.

Then the healing process started. I began to think of my perpetrators not as beasts and demons but as human beings who, like me, need the power of God to transform their hearts. These fellow countrymen and I were created in God's image to share the land, the country, the air and a future. Healing started when my imperfect forgiveness was offered. It was a beginning of the journey toward reconciliation on which I continue to work not only for myself but also for my fellow countrymen—Hutus and Tutsis—and for the African communities.

BACK FROM THE DEAD

Six months after I had mourned and lamented the death of my family and church members, I was in Kampala training Hutu and Tutsi church leaders from Rwanda and from the Hutu refugee camps in eastern Congo. While there, I received the news that my mother and my niece were alive. They had been living in the forest for six months. This was more shocking to me than the news of their death.

But the news was true. My mother had fainted and fallen on the ground during the shooting. She spent between four and five hours under the heap of dead bodies that piled on her as neighbors were hit by the rain of bullets. When she became conscious she pulled herself out from under the dead bodies and was covered with the blood of those who had been shot. As she struggled to crawl away toward the bush, she saw a baby crying over her dead mother. She picked up the two-year-old and went into the forest with her. For four days she did not recognize that the baby was her own granddaughter.

My mother and niece, together with others who had fled into the forest, lived in the bush for six months eating grass, roots of trees and anything else they could chew. As many started dying from dysentery, cholera and starvation, the rest decided to continue toward the villages in Congo where they would be far from the war in Rwanda. My mother was found by friends who brought her to my brother. He sent me the message saying that she was alive.

My mother was traumatized and said she wished she could have died with the rest. She was bitter—not because others died, but because she was alive while others were dead. She wished God had taken her home together with other believers who now were in heaven where they would not see suffering again.

After my mother recovered, she went back to our village and found four kids whose parents and siblings were massacred. She decided to raise them as her own. She then found the reason for her living. She said, "I now know why I survived. God wanted me to take care of these children." Then seventy-four years old, my mother continued to care for orphans in the village until she turned eighty in April 2007. Most of the orphans have grown up or found some distant relatives who are caring for them, but my mother continues to minister to both old and young widows in the community.

One year after the killing of my family and friends, I was back in Kampala, training Hutu and Tutsi pastors from Rwanda, Congo and Burundi, when I discovered in the groups three relatives of those who led the killings in my home village. As anger and resentment started to cloud my view of God's forgiveness and faithfulness in my personal life, I heard the quiet but clear voice of God's Spirit challenging me to remember that I had forgiven those who murdered my family.

The Lord told me that I had to repent and ask these three men for forgiveness. They were my brothers in Christ, not the murderers of my family. They were related to and fellow tribesmen of those who murdered my family by blood of tribe, but they were more closely related to me by the blood of Jesus. They were the redeemed of Christ, members of my family through our common adoption in the family of God. Therefore, I needed to repent and ask them to forgive me for hating them and being angry against them for the sins of their blood fathers and brothers. I had allowed my pain, grief, anger and bitterness to eclipse my spiritual eyes. But the Lord showed me the reality of my shared identity with these brothers in Christ. We all belonged to the family of Christ. Our shared identity in Christ was superior to any other identity that culture, tradition and history had assigned to us.

After wrestling with the Lord, I gathered the courage to ask for forgiveness from these men. I reminded the whole group of pastors and church leaders what had happened to my family and my village. I acknowledged the anger and resentment toward my brothers whose relatives had murdered my own. I then called the three brothers to join me at the podium where I had stood to start the conference and asked them to forgive me. I told them I had no right to hate them and be angry with them since they were not present in the village when the killings took place. They were my brothers, with whom I was to spend eternity.

The Lord was gracious. These brethren forgave me for my anger and resentment toward them, and they also asked me to forgive them for what their families had done to my family and to the members of my church and community. As we all wept, confessed and forgave each other, the Lord started speaking to the rest of the pastors and church leaders in the meeting. Some of these leaders harbored bitterness and unforgiveness toward neighbors who had killed their wives, children and family members or destroyed, looted and damaged their properties. The encounter allowed the audience to evaluate their own struggles to grant and receive forgiveness.

In the prayer Jesus taught his disciples to pray, he emphasized the daily practice of forgiveness as a way of maintaining and sustaining relationships. Just like food, forgiveness sustains our lives in the community. Just as we cannot live without daily bread, we cannot fully live our life in communion with each other and with God without the ability to grant and receive forgiveness (Matthew 6:9-15). I've had to learn this in my personal life as well as in my public ministry. But whether we hear the gospel at home or at work, I believe Jesus Christ is the same yesterday, today and forever (Hebrews 13:8). Forgiveness is the heart of the gospel, and if we are to live lives that shine forth God's good news, we have to learn the ways of living that make for peace.

LEADING FROM THE CENTER

If forgiveness is the heart of the gospel, it is the center of the church's mission as well. While most Christians cherish the assurance that their own sins have been forgiven, we have not cultivated the practice of horizontal forgiveness within the community of believers and the wider social community. Contemporary events causing brokenness and the disruption of relationships through the natural human responses of hatred and retribution call for a comprehensive Christian approach to forgiveness. We need something more than therapeutic self-help. The uniqueness of Christian forgiveness derives from its motivation in divine forgiveness and its practice modeled by and within the community of believers.

Since 1994, the Lord has continued to impress on my heart the need to equip and train church leaders, pastors and layleaders in East and central Africa who have no theological and leadership training opportunities. The HIV/AIDS pandemic has also caused a great need for pastoral care and counseling to the dying and to the bereaved families. In addition, ALARM has been dealing with issues of biblical repentance, forgiveness, conflict resolution and tribal reconciliation. Our ultimate goal is to empower the African church to be an agent of forgiveness and reconciliation in the African communities. After God reconciled us to himself through Christ, he committed to us the ministry and message of reconciliation in a world of brokenness (2 Corinthians 5:18-19).

We train pastoral leaders and layleaders from different denominations, different tribes and different ethnic groups in central and East Africa. Over the past fifteen years, the Lord has expanded our work to eight countries (Rwanda, Burundi, Congo, Sudan, Uganda, Tanzania, Kenya and Zambia). I've had the opportunity to put together a team of fifty-one full-time staff in Africa, four staff in the United States, and numerous volunteers who have a passion and vision for training national leaders in the areas of pastoral leadership, biblical forgiveness and reconciliation ministries. In Rwanda and Burundi, Hutu and Tutsi pastors are working hand-in-hand to be models of healing and reconciliation. ALARM is breaking tribalism and denominationalism while building trust and unity among Christian leaders from different tribes and denominations. God has continued to bring to ALARM new friends who provide funds and support to strengthen the African church by training and equipping its leadership. The vision has grown beyond me and the Lord has brought to this ministry other trustworthy African leaders who are now training Africans for the transformation and reconciliation of their own communities.

It has not been easy to continue to witness the killing,

torture, imprisonment, intimidation and persecution of those who are preaching the message of biblical repentance, forgiveness and reconciliation. But that is not all we see. We are also witnessing a new hope and a new role for the African church in bringing healing to hurting communities and families. Without strong pastoral leadership, the African church will not make a significant impact on the continent, which is ripe for harvest.

We envision a biblical Christianity replacing a tribal Christianity that has failed in the face of genocide, corruption, poverty and HIV/AIDS. The crisis of Africa is a leadership crisis. God has blessed Africa with human and natural resources. Our tribal and ethnic differences should make us strong just as our natural minerals and oil do. Church leaders must be custodians and stewards of these resources and must model redemptive and reconciling leadership in the community.

FINDING MODELS OF FORGIVENESS

Because I care about the formation of leaders in the African church, I have spent time in higher education, receiving training that I now pass on to pastors in my work with ALARM. I have been disappointed in my studies, however, by the limited reflection on forgiveness. Theological discussions of forgiveness have focused on divine forgiveness and its important place in the order and history of salvation. Forgiveness has also been treated in its doctrinal aspect in conjunction with the theology of atonement, redemption, salvation and sanctification. But the importance of forgiveness as a Christian discipline has received less attention in theological and pastoral writings in comparison to available contemporary literature on forgiveness from psychologists and therapeutic counselors. When it has been considered theologically, forgiveness has often been reduced to the individual and interpersonal, seen as therapy for one's own emotional healing.

This is why I was so glad to discover Greg Jones's book *Embodying Forgiveness.* When I started doing my doctoral research at Dallas Theological Seminary on contemporary models of forgiveness, I wanted to develop a new model that focuses on communal forgiveness.[1] Because unforgiveness in Scripture is spoken of in the context of the community and because my real world is community-based, it was obvious to me that theological scholarship on forgiveness should include its communal aspects.

As I read the literature, Greg Jones stood out in his call to the Christian community to embody forgiveness and build communities of forgiveness. He sounded like an African evangelical theologian, but he belonged to the "tribe" of Duke. So I began the journey toward Duke Divinity School in my mind. First, I decided that one of the three theologians on forgiveness I would study was Greg Jones. Second, I planned to visit him and start the reconciliation process between the "tribe" of Duke Divinity School and the "tribe" of Dallas Theological Seminary—groups that can be as hostile to one another as Hutus and Tutsis in Rwanda.

God made it easier and quicker for me to meet Greg than I had planned. The Lausanne Committee for World Evangelization invited me to be a co-convener for the "Racial and Tribal Reconciliation" issue group, and the other co-convener was Chris Rice, then a student at Duke Divinity School. As Chris and I pulled together a team from all over the world to serve on the committee, Duke Divinity School agreed to host most of our meetings. Not only did I meet Greg, I also had the opportunity to dine with him, laugh with him, cry with him and work with him. I learned more from him on what it means to embody forgiveness from his personal life stories. I was privileged also to make a small contribution to the establishment of Duke Divinity's Center for Reconciliation where Chris Rice is now the codirector.

Greg and I are excited to share with you our journeys. Ours are two journeys with one destination—two different experiences, but one common conviction. Forgiveness must be lived out, must be taught and learned in the context of our lives. Most importantly, it must be received and granted continuously and humbly because it is not our own. Without it, we are dead. But in receiving it as a gift and learning to embody it in communion with God and others, we are born again to eternal life. This is, indeed, the heart of the gospel of Jesus Christ.

2

The Dance of Forgiveness

L. GREGORY JONES

I am humbled by the invitation to write a book on forgiveness with my friend Célestin. Indeed, it is a gift to be able to call Célestin a friend. When we met at Duke Divinity School in 2004, he told me the story of his struggle to live out the ministry of reconciliation after the traumatic violence of genocide that not only devastated his country but also took the lives of many family members. I remember sitting across from him at dinner, listening to the story of how his mother had been presumed dead with almost everyone else in their home village, but then was found to be alive many months later. I asked Célestin where his mother was now.

"At home in Rwanda," Célestin said.

"And who cares for her?" I asked.

"A man whose family killed my father and our neighbors."

I stopped eating and stared in wonder at the man across the table. I have taught classes, given lectures and written a book on forgiveness. Here was one who has lived it. The gift of a friendship with someone like Célestin is that you get to see with your own eyes that it is possible to embody forgiveness in the worst of this world's brokenness. The temptation is to think that he is an exception, a superhuman living outside the world of petty disagreements and grudges that most of us inhabit. But like the twentieth-century prophet Dorothy Day, who often said, "Don't call me a saint; I don't want to be dismissed so easily," Célestin will not let us put him on a pedestal and distance ourselves from the gospel he has heard and experienced. Forgiveness, he insists, is the heart of the gospel. As people who have been forgiven, he told me at our first dinner meeting, "we have no choice."

Many years ago my wife, Susan, a United Methodist pastor, was appointed to a new congregation. As the movers were unloading our furniture, members of the congregation stopped by and asked to talk with her for a few minutes. I was puzzled because their conversations seemed to go on longer than the normal welcome. When the move-in day was over and the welcome party had gone home, Susan told me that the members all wanted to tell her what had happened "that night."

"That night" referred to a meeting of the church's administrative board earlier in the year when longstanding bitterness between members had erupted in conflict. A group of board members had left the meeting to conduct a separate one in another part of the church. When that group returned to announce their conclusions to the others, a shouting match ensued. In the midst of angry words, some of the members picked up chairs and threw them across the room at each other.

As Susan told me the story, I thought it tragic but unique. After listening to stories from hundreds of pastors and laypeople over the years, however, I have come to realize that conflicts like these are more common than we often want to admit. Maybe we haven't seen them escalate to the sort of violence Célestin has suffered. Maybe we don't actually throw chairs all that often. But bitterness and brokenness are real in every congregation, family and community—because every one of us is broken. We cannot get away from conflict by going somewhere else because we cannot, ultimately, get away from ourselves.

Yet Paul writes in 2 Corinthians, "So if anyone is in Christ, there is a new creation: everything old has passed away; see, everything has become new! All this is from God, who reconciled us to himself through Christ, and has given us the ministry of reconciliation; that is, in Christ God was reconciling the world to himself, not counting their trespasses against them, and entrusting the message of reconciliation to us. So we are ambassadors for Christ, since God is making his appeal through us; we entreat you on behalf of Christ, be reconciled to God" (5:17-20).

If we take Scripture seriously, Christians have to acknowledge that we are not only a forgiven people called to forgive one another; we have also been entrusted with the message of God's forgiveness and reconciliation for the whole world. We are ambassadors for Christ. This is our gift and our task. But it is also an incredible challenge in a world of genocide, chair-tossing and hidden bitterness. How do we live into God's vision of "all things reconciled"? How do we become healthy churches that understand what it means to be forgiven and to forgive, receiving the gift of abundant life while also exhibiting a powerful witness? In short, how do we embody forgiveness in our lives and in our world?

CHEAP FORGIVENESS AND COSTLY DESPAIR

The very notion of forgiveness conjures up many painful images in our minds. Célestin's experience, though far removed from many of our own lives, is all too common in our world. We cannot think about forgiveness without remembering horrifying evil: slavery in the United States, genocide in Rwanda, the Holocaust in Nazi Germany, or individual acts of rape, child abuse or domestic violence. It is difficult to comprehend the depths of pain and suffering in such situations. No wonder, then, that we are often unsure whether forgiveness can make a difference—and if so, how.

Thinking about forgiveness also causes us to consider the smaller, day-to-day struggles involved in living with others at home, in church or in the workplace. These struggles involve annoyances that seem petty but that nonetheless can sow the seeds of bitterness, as well as specific conflicts that sometimes fester into larger and more painful wounds. Though time can calm us down and give us distance to see things more objectively, it simply isn't true that time heals all wounds. Some hurts grow worse over time, consuming those of us who have suffered them and separating us from the fellowship with God and one another that we were made for.

Of course, every Christian knows that we are "supposed" to forgive. When we pray the Lord's Prayer, we say "forgive us our trespasses as we forgive those who trespass against us." We know the warning Jesus issued after he taught his disciples this prayer: "if you do not forgive others, neither will your Father forgive your trespasses" (Matthew 6:15). But so often we don't feel able to forgive or to ask for forgiveness. The hurt is too deep, we sense that the one who wronged us is unwilling to repent, or we simply prefer division to the hard work of trying to mend old wounds. Church council records from sixteenth-century Switzerland tell of a man who pretended that he could not remember the Lord's Prayer because he knew that if he said it he would have to forgive the merchant who had cheated him.

If our amnesia is not as blatant, it is often just as real. Indeed, our predicament may be more complex and challenging than the willful disobedience of a Christian who knows what practices of forgiveness and reconciliation would look like if he chose to embrace them. We are the heirs of a Christian culture that has forgotten the life-giving ways of forgiveness. In capitulation to the spirit of our age, we have both cheapened forgiveness to a therapeutic absolution of guilt and made forgiveness seem impossible in the face of "man's inhumanity to man." That is to say, we have at the same time made forgiveness too little and too much.

Perhaps each of these pitfalls can be best understood by Christians in the context of an imagined local church. Think, for example, about what might happen if it were discovered that the organist of your church was having an affair with a church member. Almost any congregation would recognize this as a sin that destroys the fabric of trust which holds a community together. The organist would be confronted by whatever accountability structure exists in your congregation. He or she would then almost certainly be asked to leave the church and seek counseling. Something similar might be suggested for the church member, though she or he is more likely to get lost in the confusion. After recovering from the initial shock, your congregation would probably begin to consider how to "move on."

Forgiveness, in this case, becomes trivialized. We encourage people simply to cope by meeting with counselors, and we encourage the congregation to find a way to "move on." In both cases, we try to overlook what has really happened for the sake of an artificial "peace of mind." Thus forgiveness has been reduced to something much smaller than the biblical goal of restored communion with God and one another. Our response to this hypothetical compromise of sexual ethics exposes the greater compromise of Christianity in our time to a therapeutic culture that dispenses cheap forgiveness. The practice is essentially ignored because it is made too small.

I should be clear that I am not saying that counseling is not needed in a case like this or that congregations do not need to find ways of moving into a healthier future after such a betrayal. What I mean to say is that cases like this help us see how forgiveness should be about so much more than simply a word spoken, a feeling felt, or an action done once and for all. Forgiveness is, rather, a way of life to be lived in fidelity to God's kingdom among broken people—which is all of us, trapped as we are by the habits of sin.

The practice of forgiveness calls us to willingly do things with and for one another so that communion can be restored. (Of course, such a way of life needs to be well established long before a crisis such as the one we've just imagined.) Being forgiven requires an ongoing willingness to honor a new claim that has been made on us, to speak with a new truthfulness and to live in a new way with one another. If we reduce forgiveness to pop therapy, we ignore its invitation into the life that really is life (1 Timothy 6:19).

But if we are tempted on the one hand by the cheap forgiveness of our therapeutic culture (a forgiveness that would enable us to "let go" of those who've wronged us as well as those whom we have wronged), we are just as often tempted on the other hand to give up on the possibility of forgiveness in relationships we know we cannot get away from. Because the habits of sin and evil are so entrenched in people, we wonder whether the darkness has not indeed eclipsed the light. Our only hope, we reason, lies in having the skill to utilize power more effectively and justly than anyone else. The consequences of this costly despair are often violence and vengeance projected on others.

To see how this temptation might infect a congregation, our imaginations need not wander any further than the board meeting where members ended up throwing chairs at one another. What kind of life together precedes an explosive act of violence like that? Obviously the people in such a church have hurt one another. Whatever happened—words said or not said, money misused or gifts ignored—the anger and bitterness between people was not acknowledged or addressed. Rather than engage in a process of repentance and forgiveness, members thought it better to build strategic alliances with other like-minded individuals, hoping at best for a balance of power that ensures mutual deterrence or, at worst, for the strength of numbers to win the fight if things ever came to blows.

We often fail to recognize in congregational life that the

mirror image of violence is what the ancients called melancholia—what we might name depression or, more precisely, despair. This is the internalization of the effects of violence. It happens when we don't think we have the strength to overwhelm our enemies or when we think Christianity equals "being nice" and therefore bottle up our feelings of being wronged until, after eating us up inside, they explode in a rage we cannot control. Maybe the distance between the church in Rwanda and the church in North America is not as far as we would like to think.

If we are to embody forgiveness in our time, we must first name the double temptation of cheap forgiveness and costly despair. The challenges of forgiveness will not be made easier by ignoring the obstacles that are particular to our age. And yet, at the same time, we must remember that God's people have been challenged by forgiveness in every generation. Augustine noted in a sermon in the fifth century that when his parishioners heard they were to pray for their enemies, they said they would—they would pray for them to die.[1]

Jonah similarly struggled with forgiveness. He understood the nature of God's mercy and willingness to forgive, but this is what he complained he *disliked* about God (see Jonah 4:1-3). His difficulty was not in understanding God, but rather in loving the God he understood all too well. He didn't want to love God because this God, who had shown such gracious love and forgiveness, expected him to show gracious love and mercy to others. And so Jonah pitched a two-year-old fit, sulking that he was so angry he would rather die than live in the light of God's merciful love.

It is not enough, then, to know God and to understand the challenge of God's forgiveness. We are called to love God so that we are willing to risk embodying God's forgiveness in our lives and in our world. People like Célestin inspire us, helping us believe that it is indeed possible by the Spirit's power to be forgiven and to forgive. We've seen it in human flesh and heard it in the stories of faithful saints and communities throughout history. But how do we learn to live it ourselves? How do we move from hearing that forgiveness is possible to embodying its reality now?

PRACTICING FOR THE BIG DANCE

I have a friend who recalls taking ballroom dancing lessons on Thursday nights when he was in high school. The instructor was a stern old German man who broke the waltz into its basic steps, demonstrated each move with clear definition and then barked out numbers while each member of the class practiced. Having signed up for the class in the hopes that it would help him impress the girls at the homecoming dance, my friend almost lost his resolve. There was nothing graceful about his jerky movements or the cadence of a waltz barked in a thick German accent. But after a few weeks of practice, the old German instructor put an album on the record player, grabbed one of the young women in the class and swept her off her feet, spinning around the room with her in graceful circles. My friend says he decided to stay and finish the course when he finally saw how all the steps came together to make a dance.

One of the ways Christian theologians have described the relationship between Father, Son and Holy Spirit is as a dance in which three persons, always giving themselves to one another in perfect love, are at the same time three and one. The love of the Trinity spills over into their love for us, people who are created by God for communion. Because forgiveness is at the heart of the God whom we worship as Trinity, we are swept up into that movement of God's love when, by the power of the Spirit through the redemptive work of Jesus Christ, we join the divine dance by being forgiven so we can also forgive. Nothing in this world is more beautiful than seeing broken people healed through God's forgiveness, learned and lived in the body of Christ, as they are swept up into God's dance.

But learning the dance of forgiveness is not easy. Our hearts, souls, minds and bodies are deeply formed by the habits of sin and evil. Despite our destiny for communion, we human beings do not typically give and receive freely with one another, and certainly not with any trusting expectation. Instead, we often attempt to secure our lives at the expense of others. In short, we are well practiced in the steps that lead to mutual destruction and death while we know precious little of the steps that make up the divine dance of forgiveness.

So, at the risk of causing the same frustration my friend experienced in his high school dance lessons, I want to outline six steps of the dance that we are invited into as we learn to embody forgiveness. Learning the alternative life-giving way of forgiveness takes time and involves hard work. It happens as we practice these steps in real community with other people, depending on God's Spirit to guide us as our thoughts and desires are being transformed. In learning the dance we discover that our movements are undergirded by God's grace, shaped and sustained by the power of the Spirit.

The six steps, which follow, can be identified separately to help us in rehearsal. But when it comes to the Big Dance— life in beloved community—they are integrally related, as inseparable as the graceful movements of two people spinning together around a dance floor.

TRUTH TELLING

Step 1: We become willing to speak truthfully and patiently about the conflicts that have arisen. This is not easy, not the least because we often cannot even agree about what it is that happened. It's hard enough with two people, and becomes immeasurably more complicated when multiple parties are involved. This is why we need not only honesty but also patience, the virtue that the ancient theologian Tertullian called "the mother of mercy." When we try to be patient and truthful, we can discern more clearly what is going on.

In a gathering that was hosted at Duke Divinity School, a man from Burundi reflected on the racial classifications of "Hutu" and "Tutsi," the distinction that had meant life or death in Rwanda's genocide. He recalled how, when he was growing up, he was told that Tutsis were tall people with long noses and Hutus were short people with small noses. This always confused him, however, because his mother was taller than his father, though she was classified as a Hutu and he as a Tutsi. These inconsistencies forced him to ask where such a classification system had come from and why it was so important. Struggling with that question in a Christian fellowship in college, he had begun to see how the gospel challenged divisions he had inherited and assumed. Many years later, he runs a Christian reconciliation ministry in his home country.

Churches are often fragmented by divisions that, like "Hutu" and "Tutsi" classifications, are fraught with inconsistency yet hard to name because they are so much a part of our daily lives. We cannot pretend that these divisions simply disappear when we accept Jesus as our personal Savior, get baptized or commit ourselves to the ministry of reconciliation. We must, rather, take the time to talk to one another about the things that divide us. This is an urgent task, Jesus insists—more important, even, than our offerings to God: "So when you are offering your gift at the altar, if you remember that your brother or sister has something against you, leave your gift there before the altar and go; first be reconciled to your brother or sister, and then come and offer your gift" (Matthew 5:23-24). Wherever we are, we must begin now. But we cannot assume that every conflict will be resolved by sundown. While we must be quick to take this first step, the response we hope for requires patience. Forgiveness takes time.

ACKNOWLEDGING ANGER

Step 2: We acknowledge both the existence of anger and bitterness, and a desire to overcome them. Whether these emotions are our own or belong to others who are mad at us, it does no good to deny them. Besides, anger can be a sign of life. We should be more troubled by those whose passion is hidden or, worse, extinguished. As we noted when looking at the pitfall of costly despair, bottling up our feelings can be extremely dangerous for ourselves and those around us. We learn to overcome bitterness as we begin to live differently through practices that transform hatred into love.

Several years ago a woman enrolled in my course on forgiveness while she was in the midst of a trial as the victim of a rapist. I suggested that she might want to wait to take the course, as it would undoubtedly open wounds for her, but she wanted to stay. After the session on loving enemies, she came to my office. "You know, that sounds good, and I know Jesus said it," she told me, "but I want the guy to rot in hell." I told her I understood that. "You talked about people praying," she said. "What did you mean?"

I answered by asking, "Would you be willing to let me pray for him for you?" There was a long silence. Then she said, "Well, I suppose."

A couple of months went by. She stopped me one day on campus and asked, "Are you praying for him?" I said yes. She said, "Okay."

Six more months went by, and she came to my office. She asked, "Are you still praying?" I said yes and she said, "Yes, I am too." I asked what she was praying, and she said, "I don't know. I just call out his name."

Two years later she wrote me a letter and said that she still could only call out his name. "But," she added, "I hope you are still praying for him." Her anger and bitterness are still real, and she's not ignoring that. As a Christian, though, she wants to overcome them and has entered into a practice of prayer in community. It may take a very long time, but we believe that the power of God is what draws us into and sustains this dance. If Christ is risen, death is defeated. Even our deepest hatred can be transformed into love.

CONCERN FOR THE OTHER

Step 3: We summon up a concern for the well-being of the other as a child of God. Sometimes our partner in the dance of forgiveness is a total stranger; at other times, he or she is intimately connected to us, someone from whom we have been estranged. Either way, seeing as children of God the ones on whom our bitterness focuses challenges our tendency to perceive them simply as enemies, rivals or threats. Now they are potential friends in God.

Sister Helen Prejean concludes her powerful book *Dead Man Walking* by recounting a conversation she had with Lloyd LeBlanc, a man whose son was brutally murdered. LeBlanc, a practicing Catholic, told Sister Helen that when he arrived in the cane field with sheriffs' deputies to identify his son, he knelt by his boy and prayed the Lord's Prayer. "Whoever did this, I forgive them," he said. LeBlanc did not deny that he struggled (and continues to struggle) with his emotions, mourning all that he lost when his son's life was cut short by an act of violence. But he knew from that day when he knelt by his son's body that his son's murderer was also made in the image of God.

LeBlanc's capacity to forgive did not come from spontaneous inspiration. We learn from Prejean that LeBlanc has for years gone to a small chapel every Friday morning to pray. He prays for "everyone, especially for the poor and suffering"—especially, we might say, for those in whom it is most difficult to see God's image. Prayer is not something LeBlanc decided to do in a time of crisis. The habits of prayer were, rather, already so much a part of his life before his son's murder that I suspect those who know him well would have been surprised if he had *not* responded by praying the Lord's Prayer. Prejean indicates that LeBlanc regularly prayed for the mother of his son's killer, and even went to comfort her before she died. Where she might have been left to face death alone, the dance of forgiveness made it possible for her to be accompanied by the most unlikely of friends.

Recognizing, Remembering, Repenting

Step 4: We recognize our own complicity in conflict, remember that we have been forgiven in the past and take the step of repentance. This does not mean ignoring the difference between victims and victimizers. People need to be held accountable for their actions. Wrongdoers need to repent and ask for forgiveness, even as those who have been victimized struggle to forgive. Even so, in all but the most extreme cases, we also need to recognize and resist our temptation to blame others while exonerating ourselves. All too often we see the speck in other people's eyes while not noticing the log in our own (Matthew 7:1-5). We tend to ignore our own wrongdoing.

What Célestin learned in his experience with the tribesmen of those who killed his family is true in almost every situation of brokenness and division: *repentance breaks the cycle of violence and creates space for God to do something new.* How can the one whose family members were killed repent before the family of the killers? Because he has learned the grace of God's judgment. Jesus Christ is a judge whose judgment does not condemn but rather brings salvation. Because Jesus himself became a human being and a companion of sinners, he has subjected all human judging to judgment.

He challenges our tendency to judgmentalism.

We cannot ignore the need for judgment. Sin is the enemy of life and must be destroyed. But we deceive ourselves when we believe that we can name the sin in others or ourselves and stamp it out by our own strength. We learn to name our sin as sin through the gift of God's judgment, a judgment of grace. Our sin is both judged and forgiven by the One who laid down his life for us. Because we have been judged by this One, we need not judge others. Because we are forgiven in Christ, we must forgive. As Célestin says, "We have no choice."

The desert tradition offers a wonderful image of what it means to be transformed by God's judgment into an instrument of healing in the world. Abba Moses, who had been a brigand in the Egyptian desert before his conversion, was held up as an example of repentance:

> There was a brother at Scetis who had committed a fault. So they called a meeting and invited Abba Moses. He refused to go. The priest sent someone to say to him, "They're all waiting for you." So Moses got up and set off; he took a leaky jug and filled it with water and took it with him. The others came out to meet him and said, "What is this, father?" The old man said to them, "My sins run out behind me and I cannot see them, yet here I am coming to sit in judgment on the mistakes of someone else." When they heard this, they called off the meeting.[2]

Our refusal to judge others is not about minimizing sin; it is, rather, as Abba Moses and Célestin demonstrate, about learning to see the need for forgiveness that we all share in our own lives. This is, in practice, the step that makes healing possible. "To assume the right to judge, or to assume that you have arrived at a settled spiritual maturity that entitles you to prescribe confidently at a distance for another's sickness, is in fact to leave others without the therapy that they need for their souls," writes Archbishop Rowan Williams. "It is to cut them off from God, to leave them in their spiritual slavery—while reinforcing your own slavery."[3] Taking the step of repentance ourselves, we create space for the healing God wants to give, for the healing that each of us needs.

COMMITMENT TO CHANGE

Step 5: We make a commitment to struggle to change whatever caused and continues to perpetuate our conflicts. Forgiveness does not merely refer backwards to the absolution of guilt; it also looks forward to the restoration of community. Forgiveness ought to usher in repentance and change. It ought to inspire prophetic protest wherever people's lives are being diminished and destroyed. Forgiveness and justice are closely related.

To be forgiven is to experience the release and love that enables us to join God's movement to set others free—the captives, those who have been condemned to die and all of us who feel we are trapped in death. Learning the dance of forgiveness in a broken and divided world will always mean learning a subversive step that challenges anything that perpetuates brokenness and division. We must not forget that Jesus was executed outside Jerusalem not for revolutionary violence but for *forgiving sins*. Only God could forgive sins, and the religious leaders of Jesus' day knew that such an act was a subversion of their power system. This is why they accused Jesus of blasphemy and, along with all of humanity, condemned him to die.

In a world where so many people have been crushed by condemnation—even condemnation "in God's name"— the dance of forgiveness requires a step that leads us to stand up for justice and extend the word of God's forgiveness to all who suffer. In the words of the freedom song, "We who believe in freedom cannot rest until it comes." If, as Martin Luther King taught us, injustice anywhere is a threat to justice everywhere, then the work of a church that has learned the dance of forgiveness will include working to extend the freedom we have experienced in Christ to all God's children everywhere. We do well to remember that Archbishop Desmond Tutu, who reminds us that there is "no future without forgiveness," struggled for decades against the injustice of apartheid in South Africa. He has also embodied faithfulness and superb leadership in the positions of authority in which he has been entrusted.

HOPE FOR THE FUTURE

Step 6: We confess our yearning for the possibility of reconciliation. Sometimes a situation is so painful that reconciliation may seem impossible. At such times, prayer and struggle may be the only imaginable options. However, continuing to maintain reconciliation as the goal—even if this is "hoping against hope" for reconciliation in this life— is important because it reminds us that God promises to make all things new.

Dietrich Bonhoeffer insisted in the midst of his struggle against Nazism that we respond to God's forgiveness in Jesus Christ by "preparing the way" for the final, ultimate word of God's forgiveness.[4] Often we are confronted with the reality that we cannot overcome the divisions within our own families, even less the enmity between nations. But we need not lose hope. Every concrete act—every prayer prayed, every apology offered, every meal shared across dividing lines—is a sign that our history and habits of sin have been definitively interrupted by the life, death and resurrection of Jesus Christ.

This is why the rhythms and practices of forgiveness in community life are so important. They do not wash away all bitterness into a sea of forgetfulness or guarantee that animosity will not erupt in angry words or thrown chairs. Christian forgiveness assumes, rather, that the Christian community, just like any human community, is broken and in need of healing. We do not gather because we're already perfect. We gather to learn the steps of faith from a God who is faithful and wants us to join the eternal dance of life abundant in communion. Good habits of forgiveness matter.

LOOKING TO JESUS

The practices of forgiveness, then, are perhaps richer and more comprehensive than we have imagined. They do not serve primarily as a means to absolve our guilt but as a reminder—a gracious irritant—of what communion with God and with one another can and should be. We confess our sins to one another before we receive the body and blood of our Lord because we trust that God's self-giving love in Jesus Christ has broken apart the logic of vengeance and violence, of repression and depression. Confessing our sins and receiving communion, we remember not only that we are sinners, but that we have been and are being redeemed in Jesus. We remember, that is, our invitation to the Big Dance.

Practicing the steps of forgiveness is not easy. Well-trained in the patterns of cheap forgiveness and costly despair, we are prone to wander and given to stepping on one another's toes. Even as we trust that "all will be well," practicing forgiveness in the present can be a struggle. Without denying any of that, we must also remember the young woman who was swept off her feet by the instructor early on in my friend's dance class. Like everyone else, she only barely knew the steps; she was not yet an accomplished dancer. Yet, in the hands of the one who had mastered the art, she was a picture of grace.

There's a bit of advice that a master dancer will sometimes give to a novice: "Don't look down; just keep your eyes on mine and follow my lead." If we think our only partners in the dance of forgiveness are other broken and bitter people, we will inevitably become frustrated, stumbling over one another's' missteps until we conclude that it's not worth the trouble. But the good news is that we've been invited into the eternal dance of Father, Son and Holy Spirit by the One who showed by walking among us that he is master of every step. The key, you might say, is this: don't look down. Or, as the letter to the Hebrews reminds us, let's keep looking to Jesus, the pioneer and perfecter of our faith.

3

Putting On Christ

CÉLESTIN MUSEKURA

*I*n my fifteen years of ministry with ALARM, I have had the opportunity to invite thousands of pastors and community leaders into the dance of forgiveness that Greg describes. He is right: we are all novices, prone to stumble in our feeble attempts at living new life in Christ. Yet, as we keep our eyes fixed on Jesus, we are elevated above our own ability, transformed by the One who has forgiven us into people who can forgive.

Whether the context is a broken family, a divided church or a nation at war, peace is never the achievement of those with exceptional skill or untiring commitment. Forgiveness is always a gift. Like a new suit of clothes, it covers our shame and dresses us up for the heavenly banquet. But that is not all. When God draws us into the dance of forgiveness, we may be so overwhelmed by the experience of a restored relationship with our Creator, face-to-face in the divine embrace, that we forget an equally important truth: our new outfit changes what we look like to other people. With a transformed appearance, we become new people when we put on Christ:

> As God's chosen ones, holy and beloved, clothe yourselves with compassion, kindness, humility, meekness, and patience. Bear with one another and, if anyone has a complaint against another, forgive each other; just as the Lord has forgiven you, so you also must forgive. (Colossians 3:12-13)

In Colossians 3:1-17, the apostle Paul reminds us that identification with Christ through his death and resurrection seals our new identity. With this new identity, our thoughts, minds, aspirations and conduct rise to a new perspective that requires us to renounce behaviors that divide, disrupt and cause tension in the fellowship. Those who identify with Christ must think and act in ways that build up the community. In imitation of Christ and empowered by his Spirit, we develop virtues such as sympathy, kindness, humility, meekness and patience. These virtues guard against conflicts and quarrels. But we never master them, and they do not guarantee no one will ever get hurt. Forgiveness is a craft we learn to practice in concert with these virtues, which are bound together by love for unity and peace in the community where the Word of God is lived out and God is worshiped.

Our new identity as a forgiven people who practice forgiveness requires a renewal of our own humanity and a recognition of God's image in others, even those considered enemies. This new perspective does not happen automatically. In social spaces that are fragmented by injustice, tribal or ethnic violence, racial discrimination, gender oppression, marital infidelity, failed expectations, and disappointment, granting and receiving forgiveness becomes difficult. Listening to stories of deep brokenness, I've come to name three wounds that need to be healed in each of our lives— wounds of the *heart,* wounds of the *mind,* and patterns of unjust *action* against ourselves and others.

As psychologists and social workers often remind us, abusers are victims before they become perpetrators. In a world twisted by sin and selfish misuse, our hearts are first broken before they harden. Once we have been hurt at an emotional level, our minds begin to think and plan vengeance. We then begin to act in a harmful manner not only toward those who have caused pain but also toward ourselves and others. Until our hearts and minds are renewed, our actions perpetuate this cycle of hatred, vengeance and self-destruction.

What I have witnessed both in my own life and in the lives of countless others is the good news that God can heal hearts, minds and actions through the practice of forgiveness. I am convinced that this holistic renewal of the person and the community is the heart of Jesus' message and the work of the church in the world. We learn what it means to "put on Christ" as we witness both the healing of old wounds and the possibility of new relationships in our new identity as members of the body of Christ.

A NEW HEART

Anger, bitterness and resentment make the heart sick. I have heard countless people say how sick their hearts are because of the evil done to them. Others have confessed that bitterness has caused both emotional malaise and disrupted relationships with innocent spouses, children, relatives and neighbors. A troubled heart makes unforgiving people double victims—victims of both their offenders and their own hatred.

In my numerous visits and conferences on forgiveness and reconciliation between different tribes, I have met many people, even pastors and church leaders, with sickened hearts. I also have seen how sincere forgiveness liberates a heart from decay and brings it back to new life with purpose and joyful service to the community. Pastor Okoch from Gulu shared his personal story of unforgiveness with more than a hundred pastors and church leaders after his heart was renewed during a conference on forgiveness and reconciliation.

Years of war in northern Uganda have produced not only what has been called the "invisible children"—orphans drafted into the armies of their parents' killers—but also countless widows, widowers and childless parents who have suffered the brutality and senseless killings by government soldiers and rebel forces, especially Joseph Kony's Lord's Resistance Army (LRA). Pastor Okoch was eight years old when he watched government soldiers hang and kill his father in the city market of Gulu because he was accused of siding with the LRA rebels. After that, growing up with hatred and bitterness in his heart, Pastor Okoch looked for ways and means of avenging his father and other Acholi tribesmen who were killed by the soldiers of the government of Yoweli Museveni. Pastor Okoch was angry not only at the government but also at other tribes that had joined the government. Even after becoming a pastor of one of the churches in northern Uganda, Pastor Okoch resented anything and everything that the government did. It did not matter whether it was good or bad. For him, anyone involved in the government—the president, members of the cabinet, leaders in the government party, members of the Ugandan army and police, and any tribe that collaborated with them—was a thief and a murderer.

Twenty-seven years of hatred and resentment left Pastor Okoch's heart full of poison. Everything that came out of him was poisonous to his family and community, including members of his church. As he told us, "For the last eight

years as a pastor, I have never preached on forgiveness because I did not want to forgive anyone. There are people in
my congregation that I hate because they belong to what I
consider 'the wrong people, the wrong tribe, and wrong
political party.' I did not wish to forgive anyone and therefore I did not want to preach on forgiveness. I was full of
hatred and I started hating myself for having some people
in my church." Pastor Okoch was becoming a victim of his
own hatred. The shameful death of his father and the oppression of his tribe had turned his heart "black and hard,"
but he did not have someone to show him the way of peace
and forgiveness.

By the time of our encounter, the situation had become
more demonic. In fact, to the surprise of all participants,
Pastor Okoch confessed that his hatred for the government
of Museveni had turned him into a dangerous person as
he started inviting God to side with him against the government and other tribes he hated. To our shock, Pastor
Okoch said he had been praying that "demons will possess
the government and the president of Uganda."

I remember vividly how I felt in that classroom at the Ag-
riculture University. Hatred and darkness were palpable, and
I began to wonder what I had said that compelled this man to
stand up and share all these shameful things. My colleagues,
Nelson and Jessica, were looking at me in amazement. I did
not know if I should ask him to end his testimony or allow
him to continue. There was a silence that I rarely experience

when African pastors and layleaders are in the room.

By this time, Pastor Okoch was trembling and using his tie to wipe tears from his cheeks. A number of participants had started weeping with him. It was obvious that many participants had joined Pastor Okoch on this journey toward a renewed and healed heart. I saw in this room a fellowship of the wounded, but I also sensed that God was doing something new for this community of believers from different tribes who had been enemies for a long time.

In his Christian life and ministry, Pastor Okoch had allowed the root of bitterness to grow in his heart. Ruthless and merciless, without compassion and kindness, he did not want to have anything to do with those he considered enemies in the community. He had no peace in his heart and he wished peace to no one; he only wished and prayed for evil to happen to his enemies. Even sadder, he had dragged the God of mercy, compassion and forgiveness into his mess. His heart was sick, his mind was poisoned, and his actions were destructive to himself and those around him.

But God in his grace gave Pastor Okoch a new vision and a new heart. Pastor Okoch had realized for the first time in twenty-seven years that he could be set free, his heart and mind renewed. As he continued to narrate his story, he looked around the room and began calling out the names of other pastors who were present. He asked them to forgive him because he hated them. He also confessed that he was one of those who worked for the dismantling of the Gulu Pastors Fellowship because he did not want to fellowship with pastors and church leaders from other tribes and other regions of Uganda. Pastor Okoch repented of his hatred of everyone, including the government of Uganda, and promised that on Sunday (two days later) he would ask his congregation to forgive him for being a bitter, hateful and vengeful pastor. He asked for prayers that the God who had renewed his heart would continue to renew his mind so he might bear the fruit of peace and love to all people.

A few men and women stood up to offer forgiveness to our repentant brother and apologize for the sins of their own kinsmen during the ethnic violence. But many of us identified with Pastor Okoch. Not only had we not spoken against the evil acts of our own tribes, we had also harbored hatred and animosity toward each other, including our own brothers and sisters in Christ. We had become haters of ourselves and of God. We all acknowledged that instead of putting off the carnality of unbelievers, we had wrapped ourselves in anger, wrath, malice, abusive language, slander, demonization and dehumanization of others. Guarding our own wounded hearts, we had refused the gift of new life in Christ.

Pastor Okoch's honesty helped us to see how desperately we need to put on Christ. Thankfully, God's forgiveness is like a salve on our wounds, healing us in ways that we cannot imagine when we try to protect and defend ourselves. Like a good doctor, God often interrupts us when we least want treatment, reaching through our tears and resistance to disturb old wounds. Whether we know it or not, this is the beginning of holistic transformation. When Jesus wants to clothe us with the virtues of holiness, he begins by touching our broken hearts and renewing our corrupt minds.

A New Mind

Paul reminds the Colossians that because of their new identity in Christ, their thought life must be renewed and refocused. Instead of focusing on earthly things, they must set their minds on heavenly matters by replacing carnal thinking with a renewed knowledge of Christ, through whom people of all tribes, races, and social and economic statuses are forgiven and reconciled (Colossians 3:10-11). For Paul, a renewed mind gives meaning to actions. He instructs believers in Rome, Ephesus and Colossae to have their minds renewed so that they will have knowledge and understanding of God's will for their daily lives and Christian witness (Romans 12:2; Ephesians 4:23; Colossians 1:9; 3:2). As David Garland puts it, "Christians should not shy away from the fact that our lives are centered on the divine things. We offer a different way of making sense of reality and a different way of living, which go against the grain of what modern society offers as the norm."[1]

It is not enough for God to touch and heal our hearts, because our minds nurse grudges and relive the pain and injuries caused to us. Our minds poison our hearts by giving us reasons why a person, tribe or race or some sin, offense or hurt should never be forgiven. In our minds we judge, condemn and execute others without even giving them the chance to clarify or defend themselves, acknowledge their guilt, or repent of their sins. Almost everything we put into action has been planned and executed in our minds. This is why a renewal of our mind is very critical in altering our actions.

Transformation begins with a healed heart and a renewed mind. Paul advises the Roman believers that a renewed mind is the antidote for worldliness. "Do not be conformed to this world," he tells them, *"but be transformed by the renewing of your minds, so that you may discern what is the will of God—what is good and acceptable and perfect"* (Romans 12:2). Anger, resentment and unforgiveness have corrosive effects on the mind. When our relationships are injured by people close to us, our minds quickly forget the good and beautiful days we have had and fix only on the wrong they just did. Soon we begin to plan how we might avoid others, if not how to pay them back or get even. Our minds ease us into blaming and judging, giving us reasons and justification for our own evil plans while blinding us to the role we have played in a broken relationship. Christians play along with this vicious cycle by responding to injuries, conflicts and violence with a conscious forgetfulness of God's desire for us to be kind to one another, "forgiving one another, as God in Christ has forgiven [us]" (Ephesians 4:32).

Clementine is a beautiful, hardworking woman whom I met in August 2009 on one of my ministry visits to Goma in the Democratic Republic of Congo. Upon meeting me, she washed my hands and served me dinner at the home of one of our staff members in Goma. She had told our staff member that she wanted to serve and care for the man of God who had founded an organization that brought her "to the right mind." I did not know this story until the next day when my colleagues told me how ALARM's teaching on biblical forgiveness was impacting families and communities in the middle of human suffering in eastern Congo. They also told me about students who were graduating that day from ALARM's Pastoral Leadership Training Institute (PLTI), a three-year program in which we train a small group of key leaders. Clementine was one of those students.

Clementine's mind had been hardened by the betrayal of her family. The day before Clementine's wedding, traditional gifts were being given to the family of the bride. One special gift was intended specifically for her mother; only the mother could receive this gift. To Clementine's surprise, amazement and shame, the person she had known as her sister went to receive the gift of the mother of the bride. It was a moment of disturbing truth: Clementine learned that the person she had called "Mother" was her grandmother, and the "sister" she had grown up with and shared laughter, tears and life secrets with was actually her mother.

Clementine had been born out of wedlock to a young teenager. And because her mom was so young when she was born, Clementine was raised by her grandmother, who was still giving birth to her own children. Due to the shame, guilt and stigma associated with teen pregnancies and children born in such taboo relationships, Clementine was protected from all this by family deceptions. She grew up believing certain family members were her mother, father, sister and brother. But the truth that Clementine learned the day before her wedding left a big scar on her heart and sealed her mind with hatred and resentment of both her real grandmother (whom she knew as "mother") and her biological mother (whom she knew as "sister").

For thirteen years after that, Clementine never spoke to her family. She hated them, and in her mind she considered them dead. Her hatred had become stronger than love. The actions of her relatives and Clementine's refusal to forgive them poisoned her mind, and the poison defiled not only her innocent husband and children but also other people around her. As she testified, she could never think of anything good, anything beautiful or anything worthwhile about her "mother-grandmother," her "sister-mother" or other members of her family. Moreover, she found no love for her own husband and children, and had no joy, because she could not think of anything except the evil done against her. Her mind could not allow her heart to feel anything besides hatred.

Clementine's mind was renewed, however, when she understood the cost of her own forgiveness and the command to forgive others as she has been forgiven by God. The journey to a renewed mind and a new way of life started with her experience of compassion from our organization. She first came in contact with ALARM through our microfinance and economic empowerment programs in which women in a small group are taught basic business skills before they are given small loans to start small businesses. Clementine was a member of one of the groups of women who were trained to be self-reliant and support their families through entrepreneurial enterprise. Before ALARM trained her in business and gave her a loan, Clementine sat at home hoping for her husband to bring money home to support their children. Today, she sells beans, sorghum and corn in a shop. Her husband works with her, and she has also hired three men to bring people to their shop and to carry the large bags of grain. The money she earns allows her to feed and educate her children. She has even installed running water in her home.

God also used a conference on forgiveness to help bring about the wondrous change in Clementine's mind and heart. Marie-Jeanne, my colleague in Goma, and ten other influential Congolese women, including lawyers, a university professor, human rights advocates, leaders of women's advocacy groups and a member of the North Kivu Parliament, had attended a two-week training on women and peacebuilding, conflict resolution, and human rights awareness in Kigali. During this training organized by ALARM for thirty-six women leaders from Burundi, Congo and Rwanda, I taught biblical forgiveness and reconciliation in the context of the Rwandan genocide and ethnic and tribal violence in Burundi and eastern Congo. Many participants came to understand for the first time the place of forgiveness in the process of healing and the reconciliation of communities. Some were challenged to personally practice forgiveness in their marriages, place of work and communities. Most participants left the training with a commitment not only to be agents of forgiveness but also to teach it to others. There was a general consensus among participants that most peacebuilding organizations in the region did not include the element of forgiveness.

Upon their return to Goma, the delegates from Congo organized and facilitated a conference on forgiveness, which Clementine attended. Following a strong teaching on forgiveness and Marie-Jeanne's personal testimony of how she forgave the stepmother who had tied her hands together, doused them in kerosene and was ready to set them on fire for allegedly stealing a slice of bread, Clementine realized that she also could free her mind of toxic thoughts by letting go of her resentment against her family. She was convicted with the truth that unless her mind was renewed and her heart delivered, she would continue to hurt her husband and their children. The day Clementine gathered the cour-

age to ask fellow women to pray for healing of her brokenness and renewal of her mind was a day of victory. Her life
restored, Clementine began the journey of finding those
who had hurt her to forgive them and love them again.

NEW ACTIONS

As hearts are healed and minds are restored through forgiveness, new attitudes and behaviors that build up communities result. When Paul exhorts believers to be com-
passionate, humble, patient, kind, tolerant and forgiving in
Colossians 3:12, he reminds them that this distinct way of
life will set them apart from others around them. Because
members of the church come from different ethnic, social
and cultural groups, there is always the possibility of tension. However, as Jerry Sumney puts it, "Whatever the reasons for their tensions, community members must put up
with one another by acting in accord with the virtues listed
in [Colossians 3:12]. After all, whatever personal differences existed between members, they have all been granted
a common identity as God's chosen and beloved. . . .
[W]hatever the offense, they must continually forgive their
fellow believers . . . in response to, and in imitation of, the
forgiveness they have received."[2]

Both Clementine and some members of her family had
been church members before her encounter with the discipline of forgiveness, but they never had communion and
fellowship. Disappointment and shame had caused physical

and emotional separation. Like many nominal Christians in many churches today, they sang of the grace of God but were never touched and transformed by it. Though they knew something was not right in their relationships, they didn't know how to address the problem, and their pastors were not able to help them. They lived as enemies even though they professed to belong to the source of reconciliation. They sang about God's forgiveness of sins, but they failed to grant the same forgiveness to each other. Both their attitudes and actions were impaired by their history.

By the time I met Clementine, she had already found her mother and grandmother and other relatives and had forgiven them. On the day of her graduation from our PLTI, Clementine's husband told me that ALARM, through the teaching of forgiveness, has given him a new wife with a new heart and a new mind. Their marriage of fifteen years has had peace and tranquility since Clementine experienced the power of forgiveness.

Why did Clementine come to feed me instead of staying at her shop doing business? Why did she want to meet the stranger who started ALARM, and why did this matter to her? When Clementine was set free from the prison of anger, hatred and resentment, she told Marie-Jeanne that because ALARM had restored her life, she wanted to serve and assist her in any way she could so that the message of forgiveness could be heard by many. She also told Marie-Jeanne that she would like to meet the person who taught her forgiveness first, because if Marie-Jeanne had not learned about forgiveness and forgiven her stepmother, then she would not have learned about it either. Her hospitality was a gift of gratitude, directed toward us only because God had used us to bring her the good news about forgiveness through Jesus Christ.

Clementine's life is full of thanksgiving to God for his redeeming love and for the restoration of broken relationships through forgiveness. A brief conversation with Clementine on the second day of my trip to Goma did not reveal any sign of hatred and misery. She had a radiant face, a beautiful, shy smile and the elegant look of someone who knows where she is going. Her husband told me that she is now gentle, patient, humble, kind and generous. Another staff member said her actions toward her family members have inspired women in the village and in the church toward forgiveness. In addition, Clementine has been involved in serving with ALARM ministries to Internally Displaced Peoples (IDPs) around Goma. Service for her has become a way of life. Clementine's new actions are characterized by a heart full of joy and thanksgiving for the provision that God has made through the acts of receiving and granting the gift of forgiveness. I counted it a great honor and privilege to be physically fed by someone who was spiritually fed by my fellow servant and ministers of forgiveness in the hurting community of Goma in eastern Congo.

Similar to Clementine, a new mind and heart led Pastor

Okoch to new actions. When he finished his long speech of confession and forgiveness in front of those of us at the ALARM conference that day, he made a promise not only to go back to his church to ask members of his congregation to forgive him but also to work with other church leaders to revive the Gulu Pastors Fellowship. A few weeks later, we learned that more than eighteen pastors from six different denominations in the war-torn city of Gulu had joined the fellowship. They were meeting in one another's homes, sharing food and planning an evangelistic crusade together. They also began to teach and preach forgiveness and reconciliation. In partnership with this fellowship, ALARM started identifying widows and orphans who needed assistance. Many pastors worked together to meet the needs of their congregations as they preached the message of forgiveness and reconciliation. Through our Women's Economic Empowerment Program, ALARM continues to empower women and youth in the northern regions of Uganda through the fellowship of pastors and church leaders. Today there are more than six hundred orphans of war who are being educated through the partnership of ALARM, the churches in northern Uganda and partner churches in the United States.

But the teaching on forgiveness and reconciliation must also be done through actions that build trust between former tribal enemies. By bringing together widows from tribes that killed each other, we teach these women to appreciate the humanity of each other and to learn that their future is bound together. As they work together in a business, they learn to trust each other, to support each other, to depend on each other. These women are discipled together, and they pray together for their children and their business. They are hoping together, and building a new community because they have forgiven their husbands' actions (murders that made them widows) and are committed to raise up their children in the spirit of forgiveness, nonviolence and mutual acceptance.

Mrs. Helen Akullu is a beneficiary of the new actions that have resulted from renewed hearts and minds through forgiveness. A sixty-year-old widow with four children, two girls and two boys, Helen lives in Koro Abili in Gulu. She lost her husband in March of 2003. She says:

> Before I joined the group, life was very difficult. I would go and dig in people's gardens with my children and also brew beer for money for our survival. I could not afford paying fees for my four children. Only the two boys were in school. We also did not have proper clothing for me and the children. We basically wore rags. We shared a hut with my four children and slept on two old papyrus mats with no coverings. We owned few utensils which included three plastic plates, one leaking water jar, a pan and pot for cooking.
>
> When ALARM came to our area, we formed a

group and started making beads, and with the income from the beads I have managed to do the following: my children are all in school; my eldest son finished a course in building and construction and is now supporting the family as well; my other son who was in secondary school unfortunately died in a motor accident in May, but he was in school too. I have been able to purchase most of the basic essentials such as utensils, mattresses, blankets, sheets and clothes for my family. We also eat well nowadays.

New actions were also taken in building the capacity of the churches in northern Uganda so that the message of forgiveness and reconciliation will continue to expand to different communities. After conducting a couple of leadership and reconciliation seminars in the Gulu and Arua regions of northern Uganda, church leaders in these regions requested that untrained pastors and leaders be trained in pastoral ministry, church leadership, conflict resolution and forgiveness. ALARM Uganda therefore established the second Pastoral Leadership Training Institute (PLTI) in Gulu, which graduated eighty-six pastors from different denominations and tribes.

EVEN ME AND MY COMMUNITY?

When Paul instructs and commands Colossians to put to death sins of desire such as immorality, impurity, lust, evil desires and greed (Colossians 3:5) and to get rid of sins like anger, rage, malice, slander, filthy language and lies (Colossians 3:8-9), he is aware that the practice of these vices brings destruction to a community by their natural consequences and by God's judgment on those who practice them. When our hearts and minds are wounded, we inevitably hurt the people around us, causing them to put up walls of defensiveness. Sin doesn't only hurt the sinner. It also destroys human community.

As we can see in the lives of both Pastor Okoch and Clementine, anger began the process that led to hatred, resentment and unforgiveness. When a community of believers harbors anger, a root of bitterness is planted, and many will be defiled. Pastor Okoch and Clementine were not the only ones affected by their unforgiveness and resentment. Their relatives, immediate family members, church members and communities were defiled too. But both Pastor Okoch and Clementine forgave their debtors from their hearts, and their forgiveness was authenticated by new actions. Through the understanding and practice of biblical forgiveness, these two saints are reversing the effects of unforgiveness; Christ is not only being honored in their lives, he is also being glorified in their families and communities. These two have been beneficiaries of their own gracious gift of forgiveness to those who hurt them and caused pain and sorrow in their lives. Many others, including myself, have also benefited from their courageous act of forgiveness.

Forgiveness from the heart is a supernatural act. Our wounded hearts instruct us to harbor grudges and seek revenge in the name of justice when we are wrongly hurt or injured. This is true for both those who are born-again Christians and those who do not follow Christ. Even if we try to forgive, when forgiveness is done in our own strength and motivated by mere human kindness and goodness, it is often shallow and superficial, a postponing of a sort of revenge and punishment. It may also be a social mechanism used to distance the forgiven from the forgiver. This human forgiveness can be the killer of Christian fellowship or any communion. It's from the lips, not from the heart.

Jesus warned his disciples about this kind of pharisaic forgiveness, and instructed them that granting forgiveness is closely related to the remembrance of our own forgiveness. It must be granted from the heart in order to be a healing gift, and it must be expressed in practical actions as the forgiver releases the debtors and welcomes them back into fellowship and friendship (see Matthew 18:23-35). But how can this supernatural act of forgiveness be possible for men and women who, like Peter, keep asking the question, "How many times should I forgive someone who keeps sinning against me?" (see Matthew 18:21)? Indefinitely, Jesus answered. But who can keep on forgiving when their neighbor keeps killing their children, raping their wives, daughters and sisters? While Jesus would agree that this is not an easy and simple act of generosity, his answer will always be, "Forgive your neighbor who keeps sinning against you seven times seventy, just as I have forgiven and continue to forgive you."

Living a life that is pleasing to God is possible when we take on the identity of Christ. Colossians 3:1-17 clearly confirms that when our tribal, racial, social and economic identities are renewed by surrendering ourselves to Christ, our hearts and minds engage in actions that are supernatural. Putting on Christ enables believers to keep on forgiving their parents, spouses, children, neighbors, and even the murderers of their family members and friends. Christ in us makes the forgiveness possible because through him and by his Spirit our hearts and minds are renewed for divinely enabled actions; our new nature dictates Christlike conduct. We may not completely and perfectly perform, but our minds and intentions are divinely inspired. And this is the secret that Clementine and Pastor Okoch found when they realized that they could forgive their tormentors and enemies.

Jean Batiste (John the Baptizer) is a Rwandan pastor whose family members were murdered early in October 1990 when the then Uganda-based Tutsi rebels of the Rwandan Patriotic Front (RPF) attacked Rwanda, an event that later led to the Rwandan genocide of 1994. Jean escaped the massacres in his village in the northern region of Byumba and became a displaced person, living for four years in various camps of Internally Displaced Peoples (IDPs) in Rwanda. His anger and bitterness against the reb-

els and most Tutsis increased in his heart as the war between the Tutsi rebels and the Hutu-dominated Rwandan
army raged on in different parts of the country. Jean and
other survivors of the massacres in his village moved from
one IDP camp to another, finally ending up in one of the
refugee camps near Goma, in eastern Democratic Republic
of Congo, which is where he was when I met him. In his anger and vengeful thoughts, Jean forgot his identity in Christ
and chose instead to embrace his tribal identity, which allowed him to hate, fight and seek revenge. His heart, mind
and actions were then submitted to the will and desire of
his tribal demons, causing him to even praise those who
killed "cockroaches," a dehumanizing name given to Tutsis
by the Interahamwe[3] militia and other Hutu extremists.

When I met Jean in the Mugunga refugee camp in October of 1994, he was full of bitterness and hatred not only
for Tutsis but also for all Hutus who spoke about forgiveness and reconciliation between Hutus and Tutsis. Jean
became one of my worst enemies (thank God I don't have
many this bad) and convinced Hutu militia in the Mugunga
refugee camp that I was working for the Tutsi government
in Rwanda. Even though I don't think Jean lifted his hand
against me, he held the jackets of those who tortured and
beat me when I was lured away from the main camp to
a eucalyptus forest. Unfortunately, Jean died of cholera in
the Mugunga refugee camps. I was told that he died un-
happy and vengeful—a miserable pastor. I have mourned

the death of my brother Jean, and I have found peace with him as I forgave him even before his death.

Putting to death all vices that destroy community and putting on Christ will enable Christians to become agents of forgiveness who build communities of forgiveness and hope in places of brokenness. Genocide against Tutsis and moderate Hutus in my home country of Rwanda, the massacres of Burundian Hutus by Tutsis, the killing of innocent Congolese people by both Hutu militia and vengeful Tutsi soldiers and rebels, the massacres of Tutsi Banyamulenge by Hutu militia and Mai Mai rebels, the massacres of black Christians and animists in southern Sudan by the Khartoum government, the genocide of black Darfurians by Arab Janjaweed and the Arab-dominated government of Khartoum, the massacres of northern Ugandans by both government soldiers and rebels of the LRA, the killing of more than twelve hundred Kenyans by brutal tribal clashes and policemen—all of these heinous acts in our time call the Christian community to examine its message of forgiveness in a world full of anger and revenge. Could it be that what the world needs most today is communities that embody forgiveness? How might we produce more Clementines and Okochs? How do we help the Jean Batistes whose pain, anger and vengeance has turned them into what they first hated?

The message of forgiveness is needed today more than ever before. The Christian community needs an army of forgiveness in order to bring hope and healing to our hurting communities. I am glad I am already enlisted, and I will continue to enlist others. In our world of brokenness and division, this is what it means to "put on Christ"—to wear the uniform of forgiveness in the battle for the hearts, minds and actions of broken people who are, whatever their story, never beyond redemption.

4

Healing the Wounds of Memory

L. GREGORY JONES

I am struck by Célestin's description of his fellow pastor from Rwanda, Jean Batiste: "He forgot his identity in Christ." It's a tragic description, but one that is all too true of many of us in our struggle to forgive and be forgiven. There is a forgetfulness at the heart of the story of God's people. "Take care that you do not forget the LORD your God," Moses instructed Israel (Deuteronomy 8:11). But we know the tragic story of how God's people have indeed, time and again, forgotten the Lord. As Paul reminded the Corinthians, our forefathers and mothers were *all* under the cloud when they came out of Egypt. They *all* came through the Red Sea. They *all* ate the bread that fell down from heaven. But somehow, God was not pleased with most of them. Somehow, they forgot their Lord (see 1 Corinthians 10:1-5).

Such a story would almost seem strange if it weren't for the fact that all of us know by experience how our memories are compromised by sin. "The Israelites did not remember the LORD their God," we read in Judges 8:34— and we know it is true of us as well. The rich forget the poor, adulterers forget their spouses, the proud forget their place, and disciples forget their Master. Theology teaches us that our memory is compromised from the start. That is to say, remembering (and forgetting) is not simply a matter of choice. They are capacities within us that need to be redeemed, together with the whole creation.

Both because we've inherited a sinful nature and because we've participated in broken relationships and institutions, we have learned to see what we want to see, forgetting the rest in many cases. At times we also pretend that we have not seen or done what we know we have in fact seen or done. As Augustine wrote in his *Confessions*, "I had known it [my iniquity], but acted as though I knew it not—I winked at it and forgot it."[1] We have a remarkable capacity for forgetting God and our responsibility to others; we also learn to forget our sins so we can live more comfortably with ourselves.

This forgetfulness, I believe, has everything to do with the wounds of memory that we confront when we are learning to practice forgiveness. When we as Christians think seriously about forgiveness, we have to acknowledge that its relationship to memory is not as simple as we often suggest with the cliché "forgive and forget." Of course, there is a certain measure of wisdom in this folk proverb, which has enabled it to endure and be passed on from generation to generation. We know there's a danger in saying we forgive someone while remembering their offense in case we need to use it against them in the future. (When we're honest, we also know that this isn't really forgiveness.) But "forgive and forget" seems to suggest that forgiving is the hard part, while forgetting will take care of itself. Unfortunately, our capacity to remember well is just as compromised by sin as our will to forgive. If we are serious about the practice of forgiveness, we must attend to the wounds of memory and consider how they are healed in Christ.

As Célestin has already suggested, forgiveness is a complicated process involving our hearts, minds and actions— indeed, our whole being as humans in community. In this chapter, I want to consider the theological significance of memory being included in that healing process, as I believe that forgiveness is bound up with learning to remember well. To suggest to many victims that they simply forget the wrongs done to them is to present them with a seemingly impossible task. How can they forget the horrifying presence of memories that terrorize them night and day? Pastor Okoch cannot forget his father's murder any more than Jean Batiste could forget the wrongs done to his people. And yet, as Célestin shows us, two very different realities are possible for men who experienced very similar traumas. What role does the healing of memories play in forgiveness, and what is the process by which people like Célestin, Clementine and Pastor Okoch learn to remember their pasts differently?

MEMORY AS A BURDEN

We all know how tricky our memory can be. Some things we want desperately to remember but can't—like where we put our car keys or the day and time of an appointment. Other memories we want to forget, yet they stalk our minds, showing up in dreams or reappearing with a passing smell in the air. Some of this has to do with the physiological makeup of our brains. We are not able to remember everything we experience. This is both a blessing and a curse: a blessing because the selectivity of our perception keeps us from being overwhelmed by sensory data, and a curse because we do not always get to choose which memories we hold on to. Think of a child struggling to learn her multiplication tables or a victim of Alzheimer's disease trying to remember his way home. Memory does not always serve us as we would like.

In addition to these limits of memory, we also know that our minds are incredibly elastic, shaped and reshaped by the experiences of our lives, both good and bad. Our habits are like well-worn paths in the grooves of our minds, guiding us almost by instinct to do, think and say what we've done before. Likewise, our minds are marked by things done to us. Consistent, loving care creates a foundation for basic trust in children. On the other hand, traumatic experiences mark our minds, searing them with memories that can often haunt us for the rest of our lives. These are the wounds we must address in practicing forgiveness.

In order to begin dealing with this issue of healing memory's wounds, we need to disentangle several different dynamics involved in traumatic memory—dynamics that all too often converge in our most difficult social and political dilemmas. Whether we're thinking about the conflicts between Hutus and Tutsis in Rwanda, tensions in the Middle East, racial divisions in the United States, or a church where members throw chairs in a business meeting, some complex web of traumatic memories exists in any situation where forgiveness is needed. Disentangling the web can help us understand the overlapping issues involved in coping with the memories we cannot forget.

First, some people have difficulty coming to terms with a single individual episode whose horrifying effects are imprinted in their memory, such as the murder or suicide of a child, a rape or other sexual assault, a devastating betrayal, or a bomb that destroys one's home or surroundings. Think, for example, about the student I wrote about in chapter two who asked me to pray for the man who had raped her. The assault she experienced, though it may have only lasted minutes, was seared on her mind in a way that has affected her every day since.

Other people suffer the horrors of not just one traumatic episode but repeated abuse, torture and other violence over time. The effects of such trauma endure in the soul long after the beatings or emotional abuse have stopped (if, in fact, they do stop). This is particularly painful when there are permanent marks or wounds left on the body, but it is no less painful—and perhaps more difficult to identify and treat— when the wounds are imprinted on the soul. Clementine's sense of betrayal, which Célestin described in the last chapter, is an example of this compounded trauma. The single event of her "sister" coming forward to receive the mother's gift at her wedding was not the real trauma. It was, rather, the compounded effect of realizing that everyone she knew and trusted had deceived her for so many years.

Further, sometimes the repeated acts of betrayal may not be dramatic but might be manifestations of a daily failure to love. A friend of mine struggles to trust other people because she was raised amidst brokenness where others consistently failed to be there for her. It is difficult for her to discover forgiveness, or to find the strength to forgive others, because she has erected walls of self-defense in the wake of repeated failures over time.

In addition to the trauma that an individual might experience either in an isolated episode or in repeated acts of abuse and betrayal, there is trauma whose effects have so pervaded a culture that they are passed on from one generation to the next. A particular person may not have experienced any-thing directly, but the traumatic memories are still searing precisely because of the ways in which the legacies of prior horrors continue to haunt the present. Whether in the Middle East or within a broken family system, these memories are no less real for not having been experienced directly. As we see in the case of Rwanda's genocide, the cultural memory of past injustices can often explode into new acts of horrific violence, even between people who never had any direct experience of conflict with each other.

People's memories can also be marred not because of devastation that happened to them but because of devastation they perpetrated. An apt example of this is Albert Speer, the Nazi architect and Minister of Armaments and War Production who, after the end of Word War II, genuinely sought to repent for his complicity in the Nazi regime. Even so, he was unable to ever acknowledge the full force of what he did—most specifically, his knowledge of the Final Solution—perhaps because he feared that he would be unable to do so and continue to live. My wife and I also knew a man who was haunted not by having done dramatic wrong but because his standards of perfection were so high that he consistently felt like a moral failure. He could never accept that anyone, much less God, could forgive him for his failings—even though to most of us, he was an exemplary person.

Finally, there are the horrors of trying to come to terms

with what has happened to someone that we love, or what has been done by someone we love. In this case, even though the incident didn't happen directly to us, it feels as though it did because a person we love has suffered either that single brutal act or repeated trauma, or sometimes because it was our own child who actually perpetrated the act(s). A good friend of mine has had difficulty living with the agonizing memories of what her son did to other people. She's been haunted, she told me, as if she had been responsible herself.

People may suffer from one or more of these diverse forms of haunting memories. They present different yet overlapping challenges, depending on the degree to which the memories reside in a person's mind or are found in social and political traditions. In situations where forgiveness is needed, our memories converge to shape our attitudes and postures toward other people. How can we move toward reconciliation with former enemies if we are held captive by the memory of their violence toward us or our people? How can we live together with those we've hurt if the pain of our injustice to them is always on our minds? How can we navigate daily life with people who have hardened their hearts in self-defense or self-denial, and how can we guard against doing so ourselves? No, we cannot simply forget. But when our memories have become a burden, the practice of forgiveness does invite us to learn how to remember our pasts differently.

FORGIVENESS AND MEMORY

Christian living is clearly grounded in and linked to practices of remembering well—remembering God, remembering our forgiven sin as a protection against sin, remembering our vocation to love God and neighbor. In this sense, our life in God is shaped by the crucified and risen Christ whose forgiveness re-members us as a body. At the heart of our learning to remember well, then, is learning to be forgiven by God. When we are restored to relationship with our Creator, part of what we get back—part of the creation that is redeemed—is our memory. But what are we to do if some of the events recorded in our memory are things we would rather forget—traumatic experiences like those outlined above? Does anything ease the pain of those memories that haunt us, sometimes paralyzing our best-intentioned efforts at reconciliation?

Here we confront the complexity of memory, where our tendency to forget what we should remember is connected to our tendency to remember and dwell on things we ought to forget. Our tendency to remember what we ought to forget is often rooted in our desire to wallow in anger and bitterness over hurts suffered, grievances unheard or offenses unforgiven. Unable to remember well, we struggle with the memories we cannot or choose not to forget. We cannot accept forgiveness for ourselves. Like Mary at the tomb after Jesus' resurrection, some of us are haunted by the memory of abandonment. "Where was God?" we ask as we remember trauma we experienced while vulnerable. Like Peter by the fire, others of us cannot forget our own betrayal. Hating ourselves, we become convinced that God must hate us too. Like Cain, who was unable to master the sin lurking at the door, some of us refuse to repent. "I did what I had to do," we insist. Or, like Jonah, we may be consumed with hostility because our enemies *do* repent and are forgiven by a gracious God. Whatever the situation and history of our sin, God engages with our particular pasts, seeking to redeem them for renewed life in the future.

And here, I believe, is precisely where forgiveness and memory must meet. If forgiveness is to set us free for new life in Christ, it must also somehow redeem our past. As Rowan Williams has written so well, "If forgiveness is liberation, it is also a recovery of the past in hope, a return of memory, in which what is potentially threatening, destructive, despair-inducing in the past is transfigured into the ground of hope."[2] This occurs as the risen Christ returns to those who crucified him with a judgment that does not condemn but instead offers the hope found in new life. But it is a hope that comes through the return of memory, not its erasure or denial. Christ redeems the past; he does not undo it. Because of the offer of new life in Christ, the past—whatever it is—can be borne.

In his book *Exclusion and Embrace,* Miroslav Volf offers a rich, complex and profound set of suggestions about the "affliction of memory" and the potential significance of forgetting—or, as he (to my mind more accurately) puts it, the significance of a "divine gift of non-remembering."[3] Volf describes well the dangers of forgetting and the importance of learning to remember well as a sign of our forgiveness and reconciliation with God and others. The "certain kind of forgetting" that he advocates assumes that matters of truth and justice have been taken care of; that perpetrators have been named, judged and (hopefully) transformed; that victims are safe and their wounds healed, so that the forgetting can ultimately take place *only together with* the creation of "all things new."

Volf goes on to suggest that if we must remember wrongdoing to be safe in a dangerous world, we must also forget it—or "let go of its memory"—to be redeemed. That is to say, despite all we've said about the impossibility of forgetting, there is a sense in which only those who are willing to ultimately forget will be able to remember well. If the Lord can cast our sins into a "sea of forgetfulness"—if God himself can choose to forget—might it be possible for God to give us the grace to genuinely heal some of the memories that haunt and paralyze us so we can really remember everything well?

I'm reminded of the witness of Maggie, who runs an orphanage in Burundi. Like Célestin's home of Rwanda, Burundi is marked by a history of division and violence between Hutus and Tutsis. In Maggie's lifetime, she has witnessed the brutal massacre of loved ones in her home village and watched as many children of Hutus and Tutsis were orphaned by the violence. In an incredible act of both forgiveness and hope, Maggie created a home where these children could learn to live together in peace. She refused to allow her memories of hatred and violence to haunt her, choosing instead to adopt more than sixty children as her own. Years later, Maggie's project has become a village itself, offering medical care, education, job training and cultural activities to thousands of children and young adults.

When I heard Maggie's story I was struck by the fact that she had chosen to build a swimming pool on the site of the massacre that took so many loved ones' lives in her village. Neither Maggie nor the children who lost their parents can forget what happened in that place. Yet, by grace, they are able to remember their past differently, covering a place of shame with waters that wash and renew their bodies through the long, hot summers. When asked about her own life and vocation as well as her accomplishments, Maggie replies simply, "Love made me an inventor." The love she has discovered in Christ enables a forgiveness that heals memories and makes possible new life.

In this life we must be guided by the memory of sin as a shield against sin, by the memory of Christ's wounds that are healing in solidarity with all victims who have suffered and who continue to suffer. And, as Volf insists, we must remember their suffering, and we must allow that memory to be spoken out loud for all to hear. Volf believes that this "indispensable remembering" should be guided by a vision of the redemption that will one day allow us to lose the memory of traumas we've experienced, even to become friends with the perpetrators who committed them. While we need the shield of memory to protect us in the meantime, Volf suggests that there are times when we can put the shield to the side even now in order to embrace the other. Doing so typically involves the support of friends and the Christian community, a sense that the other might respond with repentance, and a confidence that we are not simply acting rashly. As dangerous as this may seem, it's moving when we see it in practice, in the lives of people like Maggie and Célestin. I'll never forget sitting across from Célestin and hearing him say that his mother was being cared for by the people who killed his father.

For two reasons, Volf's suggestion that our task is to make sure memories are "fully healed" seems more helpful to me than language about forgetting or erasing memories. First, we need to be able to maintain some measure of continuity in the stories of our lives. Features of our lives and relationships that are central to defining our identities include the horrors, the shattered brokenness that we experience. The only way in which we can still be identifiably ourselves and have even reconstituted identities and relationships is if our memories are healed rather than erased or forgotten. This is, I think, one reason why ALARM's community workshops on forgiveness are so effective: they create a space where people like Pastor Okoch can learn to retell their story as one of repentance, forgiveness and reconciliation.

The second reason I prefer to talk about the healing of memories is that, as I read the biblical passages dealing with these issues, including the book of Revelation, the vision of the kingdom is a vision of wounds and brokenness fully healed rather than erased. Indeed, erasing memories would seem to "uncrucify" Christ rather than heal those memories fully—eschatologically—through the healing wounds of the crucified *and risen* Christ.

What, then, does it mean for our memories to be healed and for us, as God's people, to remember well? How do we understand the radical commitment of someone like Clementine to remember her family differently—not as betrayers but as friends? And how might we imagine handling our own bitterness and disappointment in relationships where we would like to forgive and find new ways of living together?

The practices of the church—a people of memory—help us in this. Baptism, specifically, aids us in bearing the burden of our own struggles with remembering and wanting to forget. God's grace, signified in the waters of baptism, relocates us so we are no longer trapped in false stories and unredeemed brokenness. Reorienting our life and our memories, it locates us in "a whole new world," as the *Aladdin* song suggests, where we are set free from memory as a haunting burden and enabled, through other Christian practices, to learn to remember well. Our life in Christ is ritually signified in our dying and rising with Christ in baptism. We die to the old self, to be raised in newness of life. As forgiven sinners, we can learn to tell the story of our lives differently—presumably more truthfully—because we are freed of the burdens of telling forgetful and deceptive stories. We need not hide the truth about ourselves and our past. In the waters of baptism, we find ourselves enveloped in God's grace. Further, as we live into our baptism, we locate our lives, our memories and our forgiveness in the grace of the crucified and risen Christ.

In addition, I believe Scripture invites us to imagine a transformation in which we can learn to remember our histories, even in their ugliness, in such a way that *we need not remember them as sin* because they have been fully healed. This transformation is a process, and we don't need to pretend that it is fully realized when it has only just begun. Healing may take a long time; indeed, it typically does. We are likely to discover the healing of our memories over time as we learn how to live into new and renewed relationships made possible by the grace of God's forgiving love and the forgiveness of others.

A friend of mine once told me that he would never be able to forgive someone who had betrayed him. If I had told him just to forget about it, he would have ignored me. Rather, I invited him into new activities in our church where he discovered that it was more joy-full to be engaged in serving others than to focus on his bitterness toward his former friend. As time went on, over several years, he told me that he was focused less on that betrayal and was less worried about it. Then, many years later, he told me that he was ready to talk with the person who betrayed him and offer forgiveness. In many ways, the time that made healing possible had also sowed the seeds for forgiveness. He had been given a divine gift where remembering the sin was no longer necessary.

Even in the midst of the most traumatic brokenness and wrongdoing, we are offered the audacious hope that all of our wounds will be healed so we don't remember them. We know that minor wounds, such as that inflicted when blood is drawn from our arm, quickly recede from our memory as they heal. We don't forget them (if someone, for example, asks us if we went to the doctor and had a blood test, we could recall that we had), but they recede from memory where we don't need to think about them anymore. So also in God's kingdom, even the most horrifying memories of this life will be healed by the wounds of Christ—whose unjust suffering and death is, fundamentally, the most horrifying thing imaginable. This, I take it, is the force of Paul's statement in Romans 8:18: "I consider that the sufferings of this present time are not worth comparing with the glory about to be revealed to us." In this sense, we can anticipate a divine grace of non-remembering because our joy will be complete.

Toward the end of Toni Morrison's *Beloved*, a powerful

novel about slavery and its aftermath, one of the characters reflects on the impact one woman had on his life: "She is a friend of my mind. She gathers me, man. The pieces I am, she gathers them and gives them back to me in all the right order. It's good, you know, when you got a woman who is a friend of your mind."[4]

A large part of the healing of memories is finding "friends of our mind" in the community of Christ's body. Such friends are agents of healing and wholeness, people who help mend our lives by gathering the tattered pieces of ourselves and quilting them into a redemptive fabric. Such friends are holy gifts, and I doubt that the healing of traumatic memories is possible without them. Thankfully, the dance of forgiveness leads us from isolation into the kinds of communities where just such friendship is possible.

5

Communities of Forgiveness

CÉLESTIN MUSEKURA

*D*espite wars to end war, strategies of mutual deterrence, advanced techniques of conflict transformation and global human rights treaties, the past few generations have witnessed atrocities never known before them. Rwanda's genocide, mass murders in Darfur and the horrific violence against women in eastern Congo stand alongside many other protracted conflicts to remind us that unless a new kind of community rises up within our global community, there is little hope for the sons and daughters of Adam. What Martin Luther King Jr. said of nonviolence might well be said of forgiveness in our world today: the choice is not between forgiveness and unforgiveness; our choice is between forgiveness and nonexistence.

As desperate as our situation may be, though, we are not driven to forgiveness by despair. Forgiveness is, instead, a gift we receive from Jesus. In his prayer in John 17, Jesus offers us a glimpse of hope for the world in the existence of a peculiar community. Though called out of the world, this unique community—made up of people from every tribe, race, culture and economic status—is placed in the world to shine the light of hope in the midst of darkness and brokenness. However, though it's protected by daily divine intervention, this community is impacted and affected by the realities of the world in which it serves. Because of our adherence to peculiar principles, we will be hated by our neighbors and relatives, and targeted by the prince of darkness because of our new identity in Christ (see John 17:14-15). Our message, Jesus insists, must be built on the truth of the Word of God and authenticated by how we live. Our unity will triumph over our diversity and become the hallmark of our authenticity. And this sweet communion of the new community will attract others to the Savior because the Father who sent his only begotten Son wants to save the world from itself.

This vision of unity in John 17 is a beautiful and inspiring vision. But this unity does not happen automatically. Though God has made unity possible, the practical reality is that it is forged through intentional and unconditional love, grace and forgiveness. It is the result of hard work, of cutting against the grain of the sin and brokenness that plague us. How do we become a people committed to this work? What are the marks of a community of forgiveness?

THE COMMUNITY IS CALLED OUT

Many Christians in Rwanda were called out of animistic and pagan communities into the Christian community. By virtue of personal experience, Christians understand what it means to be called out of the world and at the same time left in it. It is a dangerous and treacherous journey. The call of Jesus comes as an interruption, an invasion. When we receive the call to conversion, we are either involved in idol worship, ancestral worship, materialism, consumerism, worship of our bodies, or even worship of our sports teams, our religion and races. Money, possessions, land, oil, finances, prestige, beauty, positions and fame demand our allegiance, governing our way of life. The call of Jesus comes as an intrusion into our private way of living whether we are tribal, primitive, sophisticated or developed people. It invades our world where we are taught to hate, exclude, even dehumanize those who are different from us.

I was fifteen years old when I first heard the good news of God's love and forgiveness from Elwin J. Kile, who was serving then as a missionary to Rwanda. Two years later I received and accepted the word of truth and became a follower of Jesus Christ. From that time on I knew with certainty that God loved me and that he had sent Jesus to save me from my sins and make me his own. I was called out of the world into a new community, the community of the forgiven and redeemed. This call interrupted what I knew as my life.

My parents were animists who worshiped the supreme being called Imana through the intermediary of ancestors, who are thought to give life or death. Before my birth my mother was barren for nine years, which she believed to be the result of a curse from one of the ancestors who was not happy with the way he had been treated after death. By offering sacrifices of meat, beer and the blood of animals, she hoped to appease the ancestor. Since a barren woman is considered a curse in the village, she could not go to the fountain to fetch water with other ladies or sit with other ladies during social functions. Sometimes the children would sing songs about her inability to produce children. She knew that if she could not bear children, she would eventually be chased away by her husband so he might marry another wife to bear children for him.

I was born in this environment, when my mother was being ridiculed by the community and my father was in the process of sending her away. This is why my mother named me *Musekura*, meaning "savior" in my native language of Kinyarwanda, or "someone who saves you from an embarrassing situation or restores your life from an impending judgment." She believed that the ancestors had heard her prayers. As a thanksgiving to them, she dedicated me to serve the ancestors as a traditional priest. I was to grow up to perform the duties of offering sacrifices, drinks, animal blood and flesh to the ancestors. My duties would be to intercede with the dead on behalf of the living so that we might have good health, prosperity, peace and good life in the community.

When I was five my mother started taking me to the witch doctors and the traditional high priest lady who would train me for my future duties. At six I started memorizing the names of my ancestors. By the time I was eight, I knew how to slaughter a chicken and a goat. I knew how to make the sacrifices to the ancestors. Like many traditional Africans, my family believed the dead are not gone but are still living among us, even though invisible to our eyes; they are now spirits who participate in communal life, doing what they enjoyed doing before their death.

This is the world from which I was called when I heard the good news of Jesus Christ for the first time. But God did not remove me from this community to take me to a place where I would be safe from the realities of the world I'd grown up in. I was called out to stay there and be a witness. I was placed here for a special assignment.

THE COMMUNITY IS SENT

Jesus asks the Father not to take his disciples out of the world but to protect them from the impending dangers of the world (John 17:11-12). The disciples were not instructed to live in a gated community where they would form a new society, isolated from the rest of the world. They were to live in the midst of the world without being part of it, without being contaminated by it. This meant they were also to deal with the harsh realities of their communities, and endure hatred, animosity, resentment and persecution because of their new identity in Christ (John 17:14).

When I gave my life to Christ in 1976, after I had joined the Baptist technical school of Cyimbili, rejection and persecution from my family followed. For the next three years I did not see my home again. My own family and village disowned me because I had given up my rights to be a traditional community priest/medium. And since I had accepted another God, my family believed that my visit to the village would bring suffering and calamity from the spirits of the ancestors. I had to stay away.

On many occasions I begged food, ate raw sweet potatoes or unripe bananas from the fields, and sometimes scavenged from the garbage. Most holidays I stayed at school or begged friends to take me to their homes. At times I worked on a coffee plantation to earn money to pay for the next semester. When I was unable to pay, my new spiritual father, Reverend Elwin Kile, would pay the balance. I even went naked for a time because my only pair of shorts had "windows on the bottom."

In God's providence, however, a poor widow named Mary in Cleveland, Ohio, learned about me through Reverend Kile. For the next six years, Mary picked up cardboard and cans alongside the road and took them to a recycling company. Every month she sent me the six or seven dollars she earned. This is how I was able to pay for school. I never got a chance to meet her, though, because she died in June of 1983, the same month I finished Bible school.

At the end of Bible school in Rwanguba, Congo, I was sent back to my village, not as a traditional priest who worshiped the ancestors but as a priest of the living God. Indeed, my world became my mission field. Yes, I was called out of the world. But I was also sent to it with the message of God's love and forgiveness. By this message, I led my mother to Christ when I introduced the real Savior of the world to her. And when my biological father learned that I had forgiven him for the years of torture, abandonment and exclusion, he accepted not only my forgiveness but also God's forgiveness for his sin. Many in my village who worshiped the dead turned to worship Christ. The light of Christ shone in my village.

THE COMMUNITY IS RECONCILED

When Christian missionaries from the West first came to Africa, many of them brought with them a very definite understanding of what it means to be called out of the world and sent to the world. New believers were called out of their communities to live in missionary compounds and mission stations where they were "nurtured" and protected from the persecution of their relatives who opposed Western religion. Leaving the world in which they lived, these new Christians formed new settlements or villages, often close to the mission stations but isolated from the world. They took literally the injunction to "come out from them" (2 Corinthians 6:17) and were separated from their people. Instead of enduring hardships, insults, hatred, expulsion, ridicule and even death, these early converts took the little light they had with them and gathered in a safe environment to protect their newfound faith. When their lights went out due to human sin in their camps, however, these secure and safe Christian communities did not know they were no longer shining for themselves or for the world. As a result, they reverted back to their traditional habits. The darkness they thought they had left back home found them in their presumed safe zones. No wonder many Christians became tribal, racial and divisive.

As a result of this history, many African Christians are committed more to their denominations than to the Word of truth and to the whole family of Christ. Because most denominations started in specific regions inhabited by specific tribes, denominations became identified with certain tribes. They became exclusive and were therefore excluded from the fellowship of other believers from other tribes and denominations. In fact, many denominations became monoethnic. Today, even in major cities that are multiethnic and multicultural, we still have single-ethnicity congregations using a tribal language for their Sunday services. In these congregations, members of that tribe feel at home, of course. But a Christian brother or sister from another tribe would be considered a stranger, if not an enemy. To the main congregation of St. Andrew's Church in Nairobi, Kenya—a historically Kikuyu community—for example, a Luo pastor or moderator would be considered a foreigner. As I understand it, this is not unlike the situation in many historically white and black churches in North America.

While the histories behind divided communities are complex, the call of John 17 is simple: if the church is to be an instrument of national healing and reconciliation, we must first forge communities of forgiveness in tribal environments, offering some real alternative to the ways of the world. What the enemy intends to use for evil could be redeemed for the good of the society and the growth of the church. As the Christian community in Africa carries out her mandate of preaching and discharging the message and ministry of reconciliation as stated in 2 Corinthians 5:17-21, we will witness new communities of forgiveness who will champion inclusion, embrace and mutual acceptance in their social environments. We live in the midst of horrific darkness, but our calling compels us to seize the opportunity to let Christ's light shine all the brighter in the world of brokenness.

THE COMMUNITY SPREADS

In a request that was simple yet profound, Jesus prayed that the disciples would be one as he and the Father are one

(John 17:11). He continued his prayer: "May [they] become completely one, so that the world may know that you have sent me and have loved them even as you have loved me" (John 17:23). The ultimate goal of this prayer is a visible witness to the world of the unity and communion between the Father and the Son and of God's love for the world. Jesus wants people to *see* the good news in the unity and fellowship among the communities of forgiveness.

In the Lord's Prayer (Matthew 6:9-15), forgiveness is placed alongside the basic human necessity of daily nourishment. Just as daily food sustains our bodies, daily forgiveness maintains the unity of the community. For Jesus, it was imperative that his disciples (and all believers after them) understand that a relationship with God is closely tied to relationships with other people. We as believers must form communities of forgiveness if we are to become agents of communal forgiveness and reconciliation in a world of tribal, racial, religious and gender violence.

However, the practice of communal forgiveness may be scandalous, especially in societies that have experienced tribal, racial, religious and political violence. My personal experience of teaching repentance, forgiveness and reconciliation to both Hutus and Tutsis in the aftermath of the Rwandan genocide has confirmed the cost associated with the message of forgiveness. It has also demonstrated the inevitability of misunderstanding regarding interpersonal and communal forgiveness. Because of pain and hurts, some see forgiveness as immoral, dangerous and even more oppressive to the victims. For others, talking about forgiving on behalf of those who were murdered feels equal to killing them a second time. But these personal and communal feelings do not make the need for communities of forgiveness less important or less desirable. The church has no option except being an agent who builds communities through forgiveness and reconciliation.

In chapter three I shared about the fellowship of pastors and church leaders from different denominations and tribes in Gulu, in northern Uganda. Despite their pain, suffering and the atrocities committed against their mothers, fathers, brothers, sisters, daughters and wives, these leaders decided not only to forgive but also to form a community of forgiveness. They planned intentional meetings where food would be shared and rotated the meetings from one church to another and from one pastor's house to another so that the whole community of Gulu would know that they are followers of Christ who love each other despite what their tribes have done against each other. These pastors also began teaching forgiveness to their respective families and congregations. This community of forgiveness planted a seed of hope in the city and region where many Acholi and Langi families had lost children through abduction or seen their village attacked and destroyed by the rebels of the Lord's Resistance Army (LRA).

Walking with this group in Gulu, our ALARM staff

have created another community of peacemakers who are speaking the message of forgiveness and reconciliation in the region. This new community is an unusual one: a blend of grass-roots community leaders, local pastors, catechists and evangelists learning together how to be agents of communal transformation and reconciliation. In partnership with the Dallas-based Watermark Community Church under the leadership of Pastor Todd Wagner, ALARM has trained more than two hundred grass-roots community and religious leaders in forgiveness, conflict resolution and servant leadership. These men and women, from different tribes, different denominations and different religious convictions, are building their communities through preaching and teaching the message of God's love and forgiveness, caring for the widows and orphans of war, providing water wells of reconciliation and learning, and teaching the youth the principles of peacebuilding and conflict resolution.

THE COMMUNITY IS NURTURED

Communities of forgiveness must be forged and nurtured by members of the community who are conscious of their new identity and their communion with God and with one another. One of the reasons why we have failed to develop communities of forgiveness is an individualistic view of life which prevents people from practicing Christian disciplines that are cultivated in community. When individual members of the community are left on their own without encouragement or motivation to forgive their offenders, even the most spiritual people may wallow in self-pity and vengeful emotions. In his book *Connecting*, Larry Crabb suggests that "the greatest need in modern civilization is the development of communities—true communities where the heart of God is home, where the humble and wise learn to shepherd those on the path behind them, where trusting strugglers lock arms with others as together they journey on."[1]

In January of 2010 I spent four days with fifty church leaders, pastors and layleaders in Goma, in the eastern part of the Democratic Republic of Congo. That section of Congo has seen human brutality due to the wars between different militia and rebel groups, some of whom are accused of participating in Rwanda's genocide. About six countries have fought in that region of Congo, not necessarily to stop the war but to loot the natural resources of a country that for years has lacked leadership. Tribes have turned against each other and neighbors have accused each other of conspiracy and betrayal. Most of the participants in our forgiveness conference were from different tribes and denominations. Their families, relatives, congregations, villages and communities had suffered at the hands of each other's tribes. Some of the leaders at the conference had been accused of being sympathizers with the fighting rebels and militia. Others had been accused of being promoters of tribal hatred in their speeches, sermons and personal conduct. Others had left their denominations due to tribal tensions and fighting; they could not worship with members of the tribe that was killing their relatives, raping their sisters and burning their childhood villages.

Monday, the first day of our conference together, was gloomy. Most of the participants knew in their head that God had forgiven them, so they must forgive. But they also knew that in their hearts and in their daily living they didn't have the courage and grace to forgive those inside their communities, much less those outside. Some of the pastors had not spoken to each other for five years because of what their respective tribes had done to each other.

On our second and third day together, it was obvious that reality was sinking in. The participants identified consequences of unforgiveness for their personal lives, their families, their congregations and denominations. They also made a list of the social and political consequences of unforgiveness in the church, especially among church leaders. When asked, "How does unforgiveness among church leaders affect the society in the eastern regions of the Democratic Republic of Congo—DRC?" each participant acknowledged that their church's witness was compromised by unforgiveness.

On Thursday evening, I had the privilege of meeting with two groups of leaders who, because of what they perceived as tribal divisions within the leadership of the church, had previously refused to come together to discuss issues in a spiritual and Christian manner. Instead, they had dragged each other to secular courts. Because some members of these two groups were at the conference and decided that they wanted to become communities of reconciliation among these fractured communities, they were able to meet with their colleagues and agree on a way forward in seeking forgiveness and reconciliation with each other and in one of the largest Christian evangelical denominations in eastern Congo. Follow-up meetings were planned for later in the year, and I have continued to pray fervently not only that these humble beginnings will result in the reconciliation of the people of God in the community of Baptist churches of eastern Congo, but also that this reconciliation among preachers, priests and prophets will be a catalyst in the forgiveness and reconciliation of many tribes in the eastern regions of the Democratic Republic of Congo. Indeed, small groups of individuals within a wider community can serve as communities of forgiveness and become agents of healing the wounds of their communities and nations.

COMMUNITIES OF FORGIVENESS INSPIRE SOCIAL TRANSFORMATION

In tribally and racially divided communities, theology and church are never socially and politically innocent. This reality calls for the Christian community to reflect on the sociopolitical implications of forgiveness inspired by communities of forgiveness. Traditionally, political forgiveness has not been on the agenda of the Christian community. For many years, forgiveness was relegated to personal piety and confined to religious life, with the transaction occurring between individuals. The notion of collective and political forgiveness still sounds like an oxymoron to many Bible-believing evangelical politicians. Yet how can we call the gospel good news in a violent world if it doesn't offer some hope for social transformation?

Sociopolitical forgiveness concerns public and group forgiveness. It happens when members of a group of offended people engage in the forgiveness process in relation to another group that is perceived to have caused social offenses and collective harm. Mark Amstutz defines political forgiveness as a public response to a collective crime which depends on certain preconditions, including truth, public acknowledgment of collective offenses, avoidance of revenge, mutual empathy and compassion, and the reduction or cancellation of a debt or deserved punishment.[2]

Practically, political forgiveness is an intentional commitment to relate honest truth-telling about the history of enmity with empathy, a commitment to restorative justice and the expressed desire to repair broken relationships. The intentionality of political forgiveness is further sustained by a communal commitment to productive ways of dealing with conflicts when they arise again. Political forgiveness must therefore deal with issues such as collective violence, collective terror, violation of properties, demonization and dehumanization of a group, and exclusion from social and political involvement. The goal of sociopolitical forgiveness is to arrive at a place where collective forgiveness allows inner transformation in which revengeful and resentful feelings decrease, while trust, empathy and mutual acceptance between groups gradually increase.

When communities of forgiveness are nurtured and empowered to extend grace beyond the church walls, others will begin to notice that forgiveness is the only remedy for individual, historical and communal offenses. In the last few years, I have witnessed the change of attitude toward forgiveness by many government community and political leaders in Rwanda, Burundi and Congo because of the work of our unofficial communities of forgiveness. Through singing, acting, teaching, preaching, and granting and receiving grace and forgiveness from each other, ALARM's Forgiven (Burundi), Ambassadors of Peace (Congo) and Reference Group (Rwanda) have caused a shift in the minds of the political leaders in these countries where tribal wars and genocides have destroyed families and communities. Within the last few years, the concept of sociopolitical forgiveness has been discussed by political activists, theologians and religious leaders as an alternative means to national and international peace.

In our ministry in eastern and central Africa, we are witnessing a gradual change and a great interest in forgiveness by community and political leaders. Christian ministries and church leaders in Rwanda, Burundi and Congo are constantly being asked to take the message of biblical forgiveness to civil and military authorities. In most cases those very authorities have caused significant suffering to individual families and communities. In July of 2006, after three days of training on biblical forgiveness in Burundi, church leaders recommended that what they had learned on forgiveness be shared with the political leaders of Burundi. One of the participants was the wife of Mr. Pierre Nkurunziza, who had just been elected president of Burundi. She told me that her husband was reading my notes on forgiveness and leadership every night and was inquiring if these lessons could be taught to community leaders and to his government officials and leaders of different political parties. Since 2006, ALARM and partners have trained hundreds of Burundi government and community leaders, judges, lawyers, police officers and politicians not only in biblical forgiveness but also in conflict management, tribal reconciliation and servant leadership.

In October of 2005, ALARM Congo was appointed by political leaders to the Truth and Reconciliation Commission for the province of North Kivu. Reverend Manasseh Mbusa Thaluliba, then the country director of ALARM Congo, was appointed to be the vice chairman of the Commission. Through our leadership training in forgiveness and reconciliation, local and civic leaders gained insights into the importance of forgiveness even in the political and social realms. Both politicians and religious leaders in Africa are discovering the role that interpersonal and communal forgiveness can play in the healing of nations that have suffered from tribal and ethnic violence. ALARM has also been involved in training Christian lawyers, judges, human rights activists, former child soldiers and local community leaders in forgiveness, peacebuilding, mediation and servant leadership.

Our responsibility as communities of forgiveness is to embody and nurture the gift of forgiveness. When we do, the world around us will be exposed to the importance and value of forgiveness in sustaining human relations and social communities. Our hope lies not in skilled negotiators and diplomats or in those with the strongest army and weaponry. These approaches alone have proven inadequate. As Patrick Glynn puts it, "Nations may cling to the angry past or embrace the hopeful future. But the path to peace and prosperity for all nations today lies through the gate of forgiveness."[3]

The Christian community worldwide needs to come to the realization that unless communities of forgiveness are encouraged, nurtured and sent out to the world, the church will fail in her mission to be an agent of peace and reconciliation. Today's major crises that necessitate forgiveness are more communal than individual. A Christian response to the breakdown of human relationships between and within people groups, tribes and countries must be communal in its approach. A united church where Christians from all tribes, races, ethnicities, cultures, sociopolitical statuses and nationalities remain in perfect union with each other and with the triune God will indeed impact our society as salt impacts the food it comes in contact with. In communion and unity, the church will become an instrument of healing broken relationships not only between individuals but also between tribes and communities.

In April of 2007, for the first time in thirteen years since Rwanda's genocide, bishops and presidents of denominations—both Hutus and Tutsis—met together at Serena Hotel in Kigali for a retreat facilitated by ALARM and two other local partners. These leaders were to discuss the responsibility of churches in the failure of Rwanda, the reasons Rwanda faces peculiar tragedies as compared to other nations, myths and beliefs of the Rwandan people about their tribes, and the role of the church in rebuilding the nation through reconciliation and forgiveness. In the course of their discussions, church leaders observed that there are still crucial problems in Rwanda; among them they highlighted the following:

1. Churches were negatively involved in the genocide of the Tutsis in 1994 in their failure to condemn it, and this has caused disrespect of the church.

2. Since the genocide, top church leaders from both tribes have not yet met so that they may jointly agree on how to solve the problems caused by the genocide.

3. The genocide ideology is still present, and those harboring it are even in the churches.

4. The genocide ideology was taught openly by politicians, but church leaders and pastors did not prepare or implement any teachings aimed at combating and eradicating this ideology for their members.

5. Many Hutus, including the innocent ones, are walking shamefully because the genocide was done in the name of their tribe.

Because they gathered together as a community of believers, a united church, in solidarity with each other, these leaders witnessed something new and special. They were able to share truthfully and in love their problems relating to genocide. In a moving service, all Hutus at the retreat decided to kneel down and repent of the sin of genocide because it was done in the name of their tribe. Church leaders who were in Rwanda before 1994 asked for forgiveness from their colleagues who came to Rwanda after the genocide because they did not welcome them accordingly in their churches. Some of the Tutsi leaders present also knelt and asked Hutus for forgiveness because of the bad attitudes they had toward them. There was mutual forgiveness between the Hutu and Tutsi church leaders. Many of these leaders have continued to work together and are serving as communities of forgiveness. Their messages have been heard from the steeples of churches and the minarets of mosques, in the chambers of parliament and the sitting rooms of Hutus and Tutsis. The unity of followers of Christ and the nurturing of communities of forgiveness will contribute not only to the restoration of broken relationships but also to a peaceful and prosperous community.

This is why I am so grateful to be able to do the work that I do. It is why I give thanks to a God who was gracious enough to forgive every one of us so that we might learn to forgive and become members of communities of forgiveness.

Study Guide

Questions for Personal Reflection or Group Discussion

CHAPTER 1: THE HEART OF THE GOSPEL

1. What comes to mind when you hear the word *forgiveness?* How is it an individual endeavor? How is it communal? How is it daily?

2. Célestin mentions both sins of commission and sins of omission. What sins of commission and omission have you committed? How have you received forgiveness?

3. How is Célestin challenged by the murder of his own family? What does he learn about forgiveness through this tragedy?

4. How are Jesus' actions on the cross a model for forgiveness?

5. What does forgiveness redeem us from? What does forgiveness redeem us to?

6. Célestin writes of the kin of those who murdered his family, "Our shared identity in Christ was superior to any other identity that culture, tradition and history had assigned to us." What does this mean? What would it look like to live this out in your own life?

7. When have you experienced a wrong done against you or the ones you love? How might you begin to offer the "imperfect forgiveness" that Célestin describes?

CHAPTER 2: THE DANCE OF FORGIVENESS

1. How is forgiveness at the heart of the gospel?

2. How have we made forgiveness simultaneously too easy and too hard? In other words, what are "cheap forgiveness" and "costly despair"?

3. Greg writes of one church, "Rather than engage in a process of repentance and forgiveness, members thought it better to build strategic alliances with other like-minded individuals, hoping at best for a balance of power that ensures mutual deterrence or, at worst, for the strength of numbers to win the fight if things ever came to blows." How have you

seen this in your own life, congregation, city and nation?

4. How is prayer a part of forgiveness?

5. How are forgiveness and justice related?

6. Greg suggests six steps that make up the dance of forgiveness. Which is the hardest for you? What are specific ways you might practice one or more of these steps in your daily life?

CHAPTER 3: PUTTING ON CHRIST

1. What characterizes the "new identity" we receive when we "put on" Christ? When have you seen this sort of change in yourself or others?

2. What do a broken heart and a hardened heart look like? Where do you see heart-sickness in yourself or your community?

3. What can we learn from Clementine's story? In what ways do you need a new mind?

4. How did heart and mind renewal in Clementine and Pastor Okoch produce new actions and ways of life?

5. How does giving or withholding forgiveness affect the

whole community? Where is your community polluted by unforgiveness? What might your community do to open the door for renewal in those areas?

Chapter 4: Healing the Wounds of Memory

1. What is helpful and unhelpful about the cliché "forgive and forget"?

2. Greg describes six types of traumatic memory. What are they? Which, if any, of these types of memories have you experienced?

3. What does Greg mean when he says we must "learn to remember [our] pasts differently"? What does it mean to "remember well"?

4. What is the "grace of non-remembering"? When can it be experienced? How is it different from forgetting?

5. Begin to imagine ways that you might retell your own stories of hurt and betrayal. How, if at all, do you see God working to heal your traumatic memories, both individual and communal?

CHAPTER 5: COMMUNITIES OF FORGIVENESS

1. How did Jesus' call interrupt Célestin's way of living? How has Jesus' call interrupted your way of living? Where in your life do you need to allow for more interruption?

2. How is your church or community formed by racial or ethnic divisions? How might your church offer an alternative to the ways of the world?

3. What examples does Célestin give of "communities of forgiveness"? How might your church or community form or participate in communities of forgiveness?

4. How is forgiveness a communal endeavor and not just an individual one?

5. What is political forgiveness? To what sorts of political forgiveness might your church or community be called?

6. How has reading this book changed or enhanced your understanding of forgiveness? What practices will you incorporate into your life after reading this book?

Acknowledgments

$\mathcal{W}$e (Célestin and Greg) are indebted to Emmanuel
Katongole and Chris Rice for the invitation to write a book
in this series they are coediting. We are also thankful for
the work of the Center for Reconciliation, which Chris
and Emmanuel codirect, that has brought us together into
friendship and now coauthorship. It has been a pleasure and
an honor for each of us to work and write with the other.

We are deeply grateful to Jonathan Wilson-Hartgrove
for his extraordinary work on this project. He has worked
with us from the beginning, helping to shape the form and
vision of the book and then helping craft our ideas into
coherent and often elegant prose. Given the chaos of our
schedules, we would not have been able to finish the book
without Jonathan's steady, persistent, faithful and eloquent
assistance.

I (Célestin) would like to express special thanks to my colleagues and coworkers at African Leadership and Reconciliation Ministries (ALARM, Inc.) who have encouraged me and have allowed me to learn from their fellow countrymen the impact of forgiveness in their communities through their ministries. Finally, words cannot adequately express my gratitude to my dear wife, Bernadette Bankundiye Musekura, and to our children, Providence, Prudence, Samuel and Emmanuel, who have been fellow sojourners and encouragers on the journey of forgiveness. Without their support, I would not have learned through personal experiences what I have shared in these pages. Because of their sacrifices, I have spent weeks and months away from them so that I can help build communities of forgiveness in East and central Africa.

I (Greg) am grateful to my colleagues and students at Duke Divinity School and beyond, with whom I have been able to share conversations about the challenges and opportunities and blessings of Christian forgiveness. I am especially thankful for the love, forgiveness and grace of my wife, the Reverend Susan Pendleton Jones. Our lives and vocations have intersected in profoundly rich and beautiful ways, and our many experiences of shared leadership in workshops and retreats on forgiveness have significantly informed these chapters. My deep appreciation extends also to our children, Nathan, Ben and Sarah, for their love and patience with their dad, their insights in our travels to fascinating contexts of brokenness and forgiveness, and their (sometimes forced) willingness to sit through more sermons and workshops on forgiveness than any children ought to have to endure. I hope I have learned through these relationships to forgive as richly as I have been forgiven.

Notes

Chapter 1: The Heart of the Gospel

[1]See Célestin Musekura, *An Assessment of Contemporary Models of Forgiveness* (New York: Peter Lang, 2010).

Chapter 2: The Dance of Forgiveness

[1]Cited in William Harmless, *Augustine and the Catechumenate* (Collegeville, Minn.: Liturgical Press, 1995), pp. 290-91.

[2]Benedicta Ward, *The Sayings of the Desert Fathers* (Kalamazoo, Mich.: Cistercian, 1984), pp. 138-39.

[3]Rowan Williams, *Where God Happens* (Boston: New Seeds Books, 2005), p. 23.

[4]See *Ethics* 1.4.

Chapter 3: Putting On Christ

[1]David E. Garland, *The NIV Application Commentary* (Grand Rapids: Zondervan, 1998), p. 215.

[2]Jerry L. Sumney, *Colossians: A Commentary* (Louisville, Ky.: Westminster John Knox, 2008), p. 216.

[3]A Kinyarwanda word, *interahamwe* literally means those who work or attack together, with one purpose. The noun comes from two words. The first is the verb *gutera* which can be translated as "to step in, to aim at" or "to attack." The second word is *hamwe* which means "together" or "in oneness of purpose." Historically the word could mean any group (cooperative, farmers, shepherds or business people) working together to achieve something for mutual support and unity of purpose.

After the introduction of a multiparty political system, most of the parties formed youth movements. The then ruling party, Mouvement Revolutionaire National pour le Développement (MRND), named theirs *Interahamwe*. As a group of youth with Hutu ideologies who were mainly uneducated and unemployed, the Interahamwe became the killing machine during the genocide. They became, in the stories of Rwanda genocide, "those who attack together." It is this group that tortured my body both in the refugee camps in Congo and in Tanzanian refugee camps because they believed that the message of repentance and reconciliation was Tutsi propaganda and that any Hutu who talked or preached about repentance and reconciliation instead of revenge and fighting for the Hutu cause was a traitor or a spy for the Tutsi government. Tutsis tortured me also because I was a Hutu making movements between Rwanda and the camps controlled by militia in Congo and Tanzania, talking to both Hutus and Tutsis when it was deemed impossible. They did not know who I worked for and wanted to know why I was calling Tutsis to forgive and reconcile instead of talking about justice, which was, rather, revenge.

Chapter 4: Healing the Wounds of Memory

[1]Augustine *Confessions and Enchiridion* 8.7.

[2]Rowan Williams, *Resurrection* (New York: Pilgrim, 1982), p. 32.

[3]Miroslav Volf, *Exclusion and Embrace* (Nashville: Abingdon, 1996).

[4]Toni Morrison, *Beloved* (New York: Plume, 1998).

Chapter 5: Communities of Forgiveness

[1]Larry Crabb, *Connecting: A Radical New Vision* (Nashville: Word, 1997), p. xvii.

[2]Mark Amstutz, *The Healing of Nations* (Lanham, Md.: Rowman & Littlefield, 2005), p. 224.

[3]Patrick Glynn, "Toward a New Peace: Forgiveness as Politics," *Current* 371 (March/April 1995): 19.

About the Duke Divinity School Center for Reconciliation

OUR MANDATE

Established in 2005, the center's mission flows from the apostle Paul's affirmation in 2 Corinthians 5 that "God was in Christ reconciling the world to himself," and that "the message of reconciliation has been entrusted to us."

In many ways and for many reasons, the Christian community has not taken up this challenge. In conflicts and divisions ranging from brokenness in families, abandoned neighborhoods, urban violence and ethnic division in the United States to genocide in Rwanda and Sudan, the church typically has mirrored society rather than offering a witness to it. In response, the center seeks to form and strengthen transformative Christian leadership for reconciliation.

OUR MISSION

Rooted in a Christian vision of God's mission, the Center for Reconciliation advances God's mission of reconciliation in a divided world by cultivating new leaders, communicating wisdom and hope, and connecting in outreach to strengthen leadership.

OUR PROGRAMS

- Serving U.S. and global Christian leaders through an annual five-day Summer Institute and other gatherings and workshops
- African Great Lakes Initiative serving leaders in Uganda, southern Sudan, eastern Congo, Rwanda, Burundi and Kenya
- Annual Reconcilers' Weekend featuring leading practitioners and theologians
- In-depth formation in the ministry of reconciliation through residential programs at Duke Divinity School
- Teaching Communities apprenticeships in exemplary communities of practice
- Resources for Reconciliation book series
- Visiting Practitioner Fellows
- Pilgrimages of pain and hope for students and others in the U.S. and Africa

HOW YOU CAN PARTICIPATE

- *Pray for us and our work.*
- *Partner financially with the center.*
- *Join the journey.* Whether you are a student, pastor, practitioner, ministry leader or layperson, the center wants to support you in the journey of reconciliation. Explore our website and see how we might connect. <www.dukereconciliation.com>

Please contact us for more information about the program or to help support our work.

The Center for Reconciliation
Duke Divinity School
Box 90967
Durham, NC 27708
Phone: 919.660.3578
Email: reconciliation@div.duke.edu
Visit our website: <www.dukereconciliation.com>

ABOUT RESOURCES FOR RECONCILIATION

Resources for Reconciliation pair leading theologians with on-the-ground practitioners to produce fresh literature to energize and sustain Christian life and mission in a broken and divided world. This series of brief books works in the intersection between theology and practice to help professionals, leaders and everyday Christians live as ambassadors of reconciliation.

Resources for Reconciliation

Reconciling All Things
A Christian Vision for Justice,
Peace and Healing
Emmanuel Katongole and Chris Rice

Living Gently in a Violent World
The Prophetic Witness of Weakness
Stanley Hauerwas and Jean Vanier

Welcoming Justice
God's Movement Toward Beloved Community
Charles Marsh and John M. Perkins

Friendship at the Margins
Discovering Mutuality in Service and Mission
Christopher L. Heuertz
    and Christine D. Pohl

Forgiving As We've Been Forgiven
Community Practices for Making Peace
L. Gregory Jones and Célestin Musekura

Living Without Enemies
Being Present in the Midst of Violence
Samuel Wells and Marcia A. Owen

Making Peace with the Land
God's Call to Reconcile with Creation
Fred Bahnson and Norman Wirzba